WHEN A CHILD HAS BEEN MURDERED

Ways You Can Help the Grieving Parents

Bonnie Hunt Conrad

Death, Value and Meaning Series
Series Editor: John D. Morgan

CRC Press
Taylor & Francis Group
Boca Raton London New York

CRC Press is an imprint of the
Taylor & Francis Group, an **informa** business

First published 1998 by Baywood Publishing Company, Inc.

Published 2018 by CRC Press
Taylor & Francis Group
6000 Broken Sound Parkway NW, Suite 300
Boca Raton, FL 33487-2742

First issued in paperback 2018

ISBN 13: 978-0-415-78535-8 (pbk)
ISBN 13: 978-0-89503-186-0 (hbk)

Visit the Taylor & Francis Web site at
http://www.taylorandfrancis.com

and the CRC Press Web site at
http://www.crcpress.com

Library of Congress Catalog Number: 97-28443

Library of Congress Cataloging-in-Publication Data

Conrad, Bonnie Hunt.
When a child has been murdered : ways you can help the grieving parents / Bonnie Hunt Conrad.
p. cm. - - (Death, value, and meaning series)
Includes index.
ISBN 0-89503-186-8 (hardcover)
1. Grief. 2. Bereavement- -Psychological aspects. 3. Children- -Death- -Psychological aspects. 4. Homicide- -Psychological aspects. 5. Murder- -Psychological aspects. 6. Murder victims' families- -Psychology. 7. Loss (Psychology) I. Title II. Series.
BF575.G7C65 1998 97-28443
155.9'37- -dc21 CIP

DEDICATION

With sincere thanks to Donna
without whose help this book could not have been written.

Preface

Circumstances rule men. Men do not rule circumstances.

Herodotus

I have never been a fan of self-help books. Whenever I leaf through one, I think that most of the advice given is nothing more than common sense. I also think that many of our personal problems could be solved with no outside help—if only we would take the time to listen to what is in our hearts and to use the intelligence we were born with.

Now that I have alienated at least 75 percent of my readership, let me attempt to redeem myself. As we all know, there is a flip side to every coin—an exception to every rule. One of these exceptions is the parent of a murdered child seeking help from grief books, homicide or bereavement support groups, and any other source available.

When parents are thrust into the horror of their child being brutally murdered—and all murders are brutal—they are thrust into an alien environment. Dazed, bewildered, and frightened, they feel lost and alone. The murder of their child evokes severe pain. Never before have the parents felt such pain, and they don't understand the negative grief emotions that consume them so completely, all positive emotions are crowded out. They cannot listen to what is in their hearts because their hearts have been shattered.

To survive their grief, many parents of murdered children need the help of knowledgeable experts. They need these experts to tell them that the terrifying and sometimes disabling emotions they are feeling are normal, and that their disbelief, rage, and agony are understood.

The book you are about to read is written by experts. Their knowledge of grief is thorough because their expertise was gained when their children were murdered and they were forced to walk through the singular hell of murdered-child grief. Each of these experts is an active member of a homicide bereavement support group. Each is committed to helping others; some by providing leadership during grief sharing sessions; some by becoming victim's rights advocates; or some by actively working to change the criminal justice system in their home state.

This book is written in honor of the brave, compassionate members of the organizations "Parents of Murdered Children and Other Survivors of Homicide Victims" and "Hospice of the Chesapeake."

Contents

Introduction

> My daughter died because of the horrible, violent temper and anger of another.
>
> *Evelyn*
> *2-6-96*

> Because of the many stab wounds and her bruised body, my daughter must have put up a real fight.
>
> *Elsie*
> *11-15-95*

If you are reading this book, chances are you are either the parent of a murdered child or someone who is attempting to interact with the parent of a murdered child. If you are the latter, being informed of two key points before you begin reading the body of this book will help you better understand its content.

First, although I am the parent of a murdered child, I did not write this book alone. I had the help of twenty-two parents whose children had been murdered. These parents reside in fourteen states, some on the East coast, some on the West coast, and some in between. Their murdered children range in age from two through thirty-eight. The murders occurred over a period of twenty years, from 1975 through 1995. Although the circumstances surrounding each murder are very different, each of the parents who endured this tragedy shares a common bond: they are decent, hard-working men and women who, prior to their child's murder, were leading what can be described as normal and satisfying lives.

Second, to me, and to the parents who shared the details of their children's murders with me, as well as their feelings of grief and the many methods they used to survive, the definition of murder is this: malicious persons chose to end our children's lives during brutal acts of violence. Our children's deaths were not the result of accidents, mistakes, or any type of negligence. They were deliberate and cold-blooded acts prior to which the killers armed themselves with lethal weapons, or, because of their callous disregard for human life, allowed their hands to become lethal weapons.

All countries, all races and creeds, and all socioeconomic groups have their share of deaths that fit this definition of murder. Many of these murder victims are children, teenagers, and young adults and, because of their youth, most leave behind grief-stricken parents. These grieving parents are more than names you read in the newspaper, or tear-streaked faces that flash across your television screen. They are real flesh and blood people who grieve for one or more decades, and some, due to the circumstances of their child's murder, mourn right up to the day of their own deaths.

In addition to learning to live with their grief, these parents are faced with the challenge of assimilating the tragedy of their child's death into their lives. Assimilating the death is a process that takes many years of hard work and effort. And, at the same time, they are struggling to restore some semblance of normalcy to their shattered lives.

To better understand the large number of parents grieving their murdered children, we need only look at one statistic. During the year 1995, 323 murders were committed in the city of Baltimore. When these murders are multiplied by the number of cities and towns dotting our planet, we do not get an accurate count of the number of murders committed, but we do quickly realize that the number of parents grieving their murdered children is staggering.

Many mental health professionals with whom I have spoken, especially those who counsel bereaved parents as well as persons experiencing other types of grief, such as the death of a spouse or a sibling, state that the death of a child can be the most devastating blow that life can deal a parent. I spoke with these professionals after a grieving mother who had been widowed several years before the death of her son said to me, "When my husband died I was devastated. I thought I was in the worst pain I would ever endure. But when my son died, I was even more devastated. The pain I felt was even worse."

When a child is brutally robbed of life at the hand of another person during an act of violence, the devastating blow felt by the parent takes on added dimensions. For example, the parents of a murdered child, teenager, or young adult know that prior to death, their child felt terror. In some cases this terror was brief; in others the terror was felt for hours or days. While their child was growing up the parents successfully kept terror at bay. They were there for their child; there to wake them from a goblin-filled nightmare and to hold them tightly until they fell back to sleep; there to sooth their child with loving words and gentle kisses as a doctor gave an inoculation, set a broken bone, or sutured a laceration. Logically, all parents know that protecting their children from danger and the terror associated with it is difficult. As the children grow into independence and "fly from the nest" for longer and longer periods of time, protecting them becomes impossible. The parents of a murdered child feel emotionally defeated at the realization that they were unable to prevent their child from feeling terror on this one occasion. This defeat feels so cruel that some parents cannot fully recover from it.

Many parents also know that their child felt physical pain. This physical pain might not have been any more severe than the pain felt by a child who died from an illness or an accident. But, because it was meted out by a brutal person who placed no value on the life the parents created, the physical pain felt by their murdered child transfers to these grieving parents as a sharp emotional pain that cuts more deeply than any pain the parents have ever known.

Most children, teenagers, and young adults are trusting and naive. They have faith in their fellow man. They have not lived long enough to lose that faith, to learn that some who walk with them or among them cannot be trusted. Some parents believe that murdered children die emotionally before they die physically. The bullet that is about to enter their brain, the knife that is about to pierce their heart, the tire iron or baseball bat that is about to crush their skull shatters their faith and naivety. This shattering, this loss of faith, kills the child emotionally. This emotional death is then followed by physical death. In many instances, it is this *double death* that some parents of a murdered child find so devastating.

Parents of murdered children can be devastated in other ways as well. Although some of us might not want to admit it on a conscious level, just thinking about the word "murder" fills us with fear. This fear can cause us to shy away from the parents of a murdered child. However, in order to survive their child's death these parents need to talk about it. If the majority of people with whom they are associated, or with whom they come in contact, do not want to think about the murder, let alone discuss it, the parents feel isolated and cut off from the world they once knew.

Fear can also cause family members and friends to minimize the grieving parents' pain. Often they are urged—much too quickly—to accept their child's murder and to get on with their lives. Rather than be allowed to express their grief openly and honestly, they are expected to suppress it. In some cases they are even expected to forget it entirely, an expectation that is impossible to fulfill.

Some parents, due to mistakes made by those who investigated their child's death or who prosecuted the killer, or a plea bargain or lenient parole board that allows the killer to walk free after serving only a short time in prison, believe that they too have become victims. Their child was the victim of a violent, uncaring individual; the parents become victims of a sometimes inept, uncaring criminal justice system. This system, although it is sworn to protect and defend both the parents and their child, sometimes does neither.

When my nineteen-year-old daughter was murdered in 1983, I experienced the multiple devastations of murdered-child grief. For several years, I feared I would collapse under their weight. Since then, by talking with other parents whose children were murdered, I have become aware that all of them carry the same heavy burden of grief and devastation as I do. These brave parents are striving to rebuild their lives. They continue to work, and to busy themselves with family and community responsibilities. They are attempting to find meaning in their child's death by undertaking worthwhile endeavors. Although it took years of hard work, many of them have even managed to inject some happiness back into their lives.

But the parents of a murdered child never forget the savagery of their child's death. They continue to be haunted by bits and pieces of a nightmare that, for them, is a reality rather than a bad dream from which they will awaken. Despite their efforts to help themselves and, in some cases, the efforts of kind, caring people who attempt to offer support and comfort, immediately after the murder and into the future, the parents never fully recover.

The book you are about to read was difficult for me to write. It was difficult for the parents I interviewed to share their feelings of murdered-child grief with me. It might be difficult for you to read. It is not a book anyone would consider curling up with on a lazy summer afternoon or a cold winter evening. It is a book written by and for parents whose children have been murdered. It is also written for family members and friends, and other interested persons, who are struggling to understand the hell that parents of a murdered child walk through, and who want to take an active role in helping those parents survive their grief.

CHAPTER 1

Defining Basic Grief

> I am constantly working with other families to help them get through this terrible thing called grief.
>
> *Mata*
> *11-10-95*

I have always been an avid reader. Sometimes I read to experience pleasure. Sometimes to gain knowledge. When my daughter was murdered in 1983, I was plunged into terrible grief. My grief contained such a wide variety of powerful emotions I felt bombarded. I feared that the bombardment would overwhelm me, and that I would not survive.

Some of the grief emotions I experienced after my daughter's death were familiar to me. I had experienced them when my father died eight years earlier. But many of them were not familiar. Never having grieved the loss of a child, I did not understand where these emotions were coming from. Nor did I understand why I was experiencing them. Because of this, I reverted to habit and began reading books written about grief.

All of these books were similar in that they each stated that basic grief is comprised of several standard emotions. The writers, depending on his or her perspective, sometimes gave these emotions different names. For example, one book stated that the emotions of grief are denial, avoidance, disorientation, despair, adapting, acceptance, and recovery. Another stated they are shock, denial, guilt, anger, withdrawal, depression, and resolution. Despite the fact that different writers used different names for the emotions of grief, the way in which they described these emotions, and how each affected bereaved persons, was basically the same.

The information given in each book I read stemmed from the life experiences and backgrounds of the writers. Some were researchers who had studied the grief feelings of a significant number of bereaved persons and then reported on them. Others had experienced a devastating loss and then wrote about their personal grief.

After reading these books, I had gained a better understanding of several of the emotions I was experiencing, but I still did not understand all of them. And so I began speaking with other bereaved persons. From these persons I learned that the standard emotions felt during the grieving process, even though each bereaved person might label them the same, can be interpreted quite differently by each person who experiences them. I also learned that there are many different types of grief, and that each type contains its own mix, and number, of emotions. For instance, a woman who suffers the death of her grandmother does not grieve in the same way as does a woman who suffers the death of her husband. While some of the emotions felt by these two women can be the same, each woman also experiences emotions that are unique to her type of grief.

During the past twenty-two years, I have suffered the deaths of my mother, my mother-in-law, a brother-in-law, and a nephew in addition to the deaths of my father and my daughter. When I combined the emotions I felt after each of these deaths with the information I had gleaned from the books I had read, and from speaking with other bereaved persons, I concluded that grief can best be defined as a loosely-knit and extremely complex process. While the core of that process contains certain emotions that are a constant, a variety of emotions specific to a certain type of grief can also be present. To further complicate matters, two or more of these emotions can be experienced simultaneously. And a bereaved person can flip-flop back and forth between emotions.

Because grief is a uniquely personal process, how one goes about working through it varies greatly from bereaved person to bereaved person. No two persons are alike. No two griefs are alike. There is no right or wrong way to grieve.

PART A
Grieving a Non-Death Loss

New activities got me through difficult days.
Christina
11-22-96

A few years ago I was involved in a serious car accident. An older man, driving a large pickup truck at a high rate of speed, ran a red light and hit my car broadside. During the accident, my 1987 Nissan Maxima was destroyed and, afterward, because the paramedics thought that my heart had been damaged, I was airlifted to a shock trauma center. Luckily, considering the condition of my car, the injuries I sustained turned out to be fairly minor. But, even so, this experience was very traumatic for me and my family.

Before my fractured ribs and torn muscles had begun to heal, I began to miss my Maxima. When I shared this with my husband, he looked at me as if I had suddenly grown a second head and yelped, "Just be grateful that you are alive. The car can be replaced. You can't!"

Knowing that my husband's statement was true, I tried to be grateful that I was alive and to forget about my car. But, as time wore on, I thought about it more and more. One morning, after telling myself for the hundredth time that I was being silly, I knew it was time to analyze my feelings and determine why I was so upset over losing a material possession. For starters, I reasoned, with buying a house and rearing three children, my husband and I had only been able to afford used cars during the first twenty-eight years of our marriage. When our finances improved, we treated ourselves to the Maxima, a luxurious car loaded with expensive extras. Over the years, we had taken excellent care of the car. In return, it had given us dependable service and an incredibly smooth ride. We were living in an age of employee lay-offs and forced early retirements, and my husband, just like everyone else, was never sure if he would have a job the following day. Because of this, I knew it was unlikely that we would replace the old Maxima with a new one—and that made me sad. Second, the accident had left me with a fear of driving. In the Maxima, because I knew exactly how it handled, and that it was sturdily constructed, I had felt safe and secure. In addition to losing that security, I would soon be required, due to the negligence of another driver, to accustom myself to the handling of whatever car we eventually purchased. I hated being afraid to drive, and I was angry with the other driver, not only for causing the accident and the fear of driving it had instilled within me, but for depriving me of my car.

It then dawned on me that I might actually be grieving the loss of the Maxima. I knew that sadness and anger are two of the core emotions of grief, and that I was experiencing both of them. As I could not recall grieving the loss of a material possession in the past, I was still skeptical that what I was feeling was true grief. So I pulled out my dictionary and looked up the definition. It read:

> Grief is intense emotional suffering caused by loss, misfortune, or disaster.

I was not surprised that the definition connected the word suffering to the word loss. But I was surprised that it included the words misfortune and disaster. As I examined the definition in my mind, I realized that my surprise stemmed from the fact that, prior to the car accident, I had always associated the word grief with the loss, by death, of a person's loved one. I had commonly referred to a widow as the *grieving spouse,* or the parents of a deceased child as the *grieving parents.* But I had never, for instance, referred to a man who was forced to declare his business bankrupt as the *grieving businessman,* despite my knowledge that the loss of his business was a tragic misfortune. Also, over the course of my lifetime, I had never heard anyone else connect the word grieving to any person who had lost a business.

I then realized the same holds true in other situations. A month or so before my car accident, the lead story on the evening news featured a group of homeowners whose houses had been swept away in a flood. I saw the tears of sorrow these people shed and knew that the loss of their homes was a disaster that caused them intense emotional suffering. But still I did not think of them as the *grieving homeowners.*

I also realized that, in our society, we expect the grieving spouse and the grieving parents to go through a period of mourning. A year after the deaths occurred, when they are still having "bad days," and are irritable, or absentminded, or cry at the drop of a hat, we accept, and even excuse, their behavior by saying that they are still grieving the loss of their loved ones.

But, unless we are mental health professionals accustomed to counseling people who have suffered a non-death loss, or someone who has suffered the non-death loss of a business or a home, we do not expect the businessman and the homeowners to go through a period of mourning. When they are experiencing the same kind of "bad day" as the grieving spouse or the grieving parents, we seldom associate their aberrant behavior with grief. We do not say that the businessman is grieving the misfortune of losing his business, or that the homeowners are grieving the disaster of losing their homes. It does not occur to us that they, too, need time to recover from their losses.

Because many of us normally do not associate grief with a disaster or a misfortune, those who have not yet suffered the loss, by death, of a family member, a mate, or a friend might believe they have not yet experienced grief. But this is not necessarily true.

I do not mean to imply that the misfortune of declaring a business bankrupt or the disaster of having a home destroyed results in the same severe and devastating pain one experiences after the death of a loved one. There is no comparison between the loss of a material possession and the loss of a human being. To draw a parallel between the two would trivialize the supreme value our loved ones have in our lives. If, after my daughter was murdered, someone had told me that they understood my loss because they had felt the same degree of loss when their luxury car was totaled in an accident, or when they had lost their home in a fire, I would have been outraged. And I probably would have thought, just be grateful that you are alive. My daughter wasn't so lucky! However, if you have not yet experienced the death of a loved one, and if you are to gain even a minimal understanding of the grieving process we all go through when a loved one dies, it would be most helpful if you think back to a non-death loss you have suffered and attempt to recall the sadness and despair you felt.

There are many different kinds of losses and, over the course of a lifetime, all of us will probably suffer many of them. While our losses might include the deaths of family members and other persons we love, we can also lose:

- treasured possessions that have no purpose except to pleasure us with their beauty,
- objects we need to function in everyday life,
- activities and pastimes, some of which we participate in for money and others we do strictly for enjoyment,
- our good health,
- a beloved pet,
- a friendship,
- a relationship, and
- even an idealism or belief that we hold dear.

For example, when you were a child, one of your playmates might have borrowed your favorite baseball or doll and failed to return it to you. A year later you lost the spelling bee at school. To you, these losses were very significant. They evoked strong emotions within you. You were angry with your playmate because he or she had deprived you of one of your most treasured possessions, and you were angry with the adult who had expected you to spell such difficult words because you had been deprived of the pleasure of winning. You might also have been angry with yourself for not being more careful with your possession and for not studying the spelling words more carefully. If you then began to believe that your carelessness was the root cause of your losses, you could have begun to feel guilt.

As you moved through your teenage and young adult years you began to take yourself, and the losses you suffered, more seriously. Your college football team lost the big game. The championship you wanted so badly went to your school's arch rival. Then the love of your life ended your relationship and started dating someone else. When these losses occurred, your life was disrupted. For weeks, or even months, you felt somewhat detached from the world—a world that, to you, seemed to be comprised of winning teams and happy couples. You were unhappy. And your unhappiness caused you to resent the happiness of the persons around you.

During your middle years, the scope of your life widens. You own a greater number of possessions and share relationships with a greater number of people. Because of this, your chances of sustaining a greater number of significant losses also increases. For instance, a fire destroys your home and some of the possessions inside, including treasured photographs and family heirlooms, cannot be replaced. Or you lose your job and, before you can find another one, are forced to deplete the money in your savings account. As you watch your home burn, or your bank account dwindle away, you feel shock, fear, and helplessness.

In later life you will be faced with retiring from your job. For a while, without a job to give your life purpose and structure, your existence might seem meaningless. In order to restore meaning to your life, you are going to have to begin participating in new activities to fill your empty hours. You are going to have to restructure your life. During this same period of time, the people in your life who give you companionship begin selling their homes and moving to condominiums in retirement communities far away from you. Their absence is going to bring loneliness.

The hypothetical events I have described evoked the painful emotions of anger and guilt, detachment and resentment, shock, fear and helplessness, and meaninglessness and loneliness. Each of these emotions is an emotion of grief. When they are felt in combinations of two or more, and when they are the result of a non-death loss that is a misfortune or a disaster, you can say that you are experiencing grief.

PART B
Grieving a Death Loss: The Nine Core Emotions of Grief

> I have had so many strong emotions since this happened. They seem to come and go and change constantly but I think by far the two most powerful have to be helplessness and despair.
>
> *Carolyn*
> *12-31-95*

> I know this sounds a little crazy but if I had it to do over again I think I would act out a little more, feel what I was feeling, cry, sob, scream, act crazy if needed rather than what I did which was to feel like I had to hold it together and shield others from my sorrow.
>
> *Sandy*
> *3-3-96*

No two humans are exactly alike. If five persons witness a car accident, each will perceive and interpret the accident in his or her own way. The police will be given five different versions of what happened.

Each of us also interacts with our loved ones differently. For example, some young adults might drop in to visit their parents once a week. Others will not visit unless they are invited.

Because we all differ in our perceptions, in our interpretations, and in our interactions with others, one person's bereavement will not be identical to the bereavement of another, even though the two are grieving the same type of loss.

Although grief is a uniquely individual and highly personal process, it is usually comprised of nine core emotions. If you have not yet suffered the death of a loved one, knowing what these emotions are, and why they occur, will help you understand death-loss grief.

SHOCK

The state of shock that bereaved persons enter into when they learn of their loved one's death is often described by them as a mental numbness. This numbness occurs regardless of whether the death was expected or unexpected. The degree to which shock interferes with their ability to function, both physically and mentally, depends on the type of relationship they shared with the deceased. If the deceased played an important role in their lives, their ability to function well during the first few days or weeks of grief can be greatly impaired.

One way to characterize this feeling of numbness is to say that it is a device grieving individuals use to protect themselves from the painful reality that their loved one is dead—until they are emotionally ready to accept that reality. Although this mental numbness generally lasts for a week or two, it can last longer.

Accepting the *reality* that their loved one is *dead,* is not the same as *accepting* the *death* itself. In order to accept the death, and to come to terms with it, they must assimilate it into their lives and be willing to move forward in life in spite of it. Coming to terms with the death is not accomplished until they have worked through the grieving process.

The feeling of numbness bereaved persons experience can also be characterized as an invisible wall they unconsciously build up inside themselves to temporarily ward off the barrage of grief emotions they instinctively know is coming.

Even though they are mentally numb, they still feel pain and sorrow. But the pain and sorrow they feel in the beginning of their grief, is not the intense pain and sorrow they will feel when the numbness wears off.

Some grieving individuals express their initial pain and sorrow by sobbing uncontrollably much of the time, or by refusing to eat or to sleep. Others suppress these feelings and continue to function as they always have. How they behave at this point in time, is not an indication of the amount of pain they are experiencing. It is merely an indication that all persons, due to differences in personality and temperament, grieve differently from the very beginning of their grief.

In addition to allowing bereaved persons the time they need to accept the reality of their loved one's death, and temporarily ward off the onslaught of painful emotions they will eventually suffer, the feeling of numbness enables them to perform necessary tasks such as continuing to take care of their families, and planning and attending the viewings and the burial. The list of things that needs to be done when planning a funeral can sometimes seem endless. Were it not for the feeling of numbness that engulfs and protects them they might not be able to accomplish these tasks.

While I was preparing to write this chapter, I asked my husband how he felt in February of 1983 when he learned that his mother had died, and in September of that same year when he learned that our daughter had died. "When Mom died," he responded, "I remember feeling pain and feeling numb at the same time. But I couldn't let myself go completely numb because Dad needed me to help him get through Mom's funeral.

"When Laurie died I felt like a zombie. If your mother and sisters hadn't been there to keep me moving, I would have sat down in a chair and not gotten up again. I met with the funeral director because they told me to meet with him. I ate meals because they told me to eat. Actually, I was in such a deep state of shock, I really don't remember most of what happened during that first week."

Not remembering much of what happened during the first few days or weeks of grief is not unusual. Years later, after they have worked through the grieving process, some people might be frustrated because they cannot remember. Their loved one's death and funeral were significant and life-altering events. Blocking them out is like suffering amnesia, and they want to retrieve these missing parts of their lives. Other people will view forgetting as a blessing; it allows them to permanently block out scenes from the viewings and the burial that are too painful to remember.

DENIAL

When grieving individuals are ready to begin accepting the reality of their loved one's death, the feeling of numbness begins to wear off. Intellectually, they know that their loved one is dead, but emotionally, they still have a hard time believing that this tragedy happened to them. They bounce back and forth between reality and disbelief. Their intellect goes to war with their emotions.

If you have not yet experienced the death of a loved one, and are finding it difficult to understand the nature of this war, think, for a moment, of a death as an injury or surgery you have had. After the injury or surgery, when the physical pain threatened to overwhelm you, you were given a dose of pain killer. For an hour or two, the pain killer blocked out your pain allowing you to be fairly comfortable. In bereavement, the emotional pain felt after a death can be compared to the physical pain felt after an injury or surgery, and the pain killer can be compared to the emotion of denial. When pain threatens to overwhelm persons in grief, their minds give them a dose of denial.

Denial is another device they employ to temporarily protect themselves from the painful reality of their loved one's death. And it can manifest itself in many ways.

For several months following our daughter's death, my husband frequently thought he saw her. After each sighting he would run after her. Of course, when he caught up with her, he could see that the young woman he had run after was not our daughter, but another young woman whose hair was the same shade of red, or whose build was similar, or who wore the same style of clothing. While my husband was running after the woman, his sorrow lifted. For a moment, he experienced a respite from pain. He remembered what it was like to be pain-free.

To those of you who have not yet suffered a death loss this manifestation of denial can seem cruel and torturous. And, in a way, it is. When my husband saw that the woman he had run after was not our daughter, he was cruelly disappointed and his pain flooded back in. But, in another way, it is not cruel. The brief time my husband was free from pain was a welcome relief. It helped him to remember what it was like to be happy and strengthened his resolve to work toward being happy again in the future.

Denial can also manifest itself in the form of daydreams or fantasies. Because bereaved persons are not yet emotionally ready to accept the reality of the death, they can conjure up scenarios in which—somehow, somewhere—their loved one is still alive. These scenarios can be quite detailed.

For instance, if your father died in a plane crash, you might fantasize that he never got on the plane. Instead, on the way to the airport, he was hit over the head and robbed of his wallet and his luggage. The robber, using the plane ticket belonging to your father, boarded the plane. The person you buried was really the robber. Your father is still alive, but is wandering about somewhere unable to remember his name due to the injury he sustained when he was struck on the head. Someday he will remember his identity and come back to you.

If you are not familiar with the grieving process, such fantasies can seem to be irrational. You might not be able to comprehend that grieving individuals can actually conjure up such illogical scenarios. In time, when they are ready, emotionally as well as intellectually, to accept the reality of the death, they, too, will see that they were not thinking rationally. And they will stop fantasizing that their loved one is still alive. In the meantime, these fantasies give them a brief respite from their pain and suffering.

Forgetting, for short periods of time, that their loved one is dead is another form of denial. A grieving mother might set a place at the dinner table for her deceased son, or prepare four servings of potatoes instead of three. In a department store, a wife whose husband died recently might find herself standing in line at the cash register waiting to pay for a pair of shoes her husband would have enjoyed wearing. A grieving sister might cut an article out of the newspaper to mail to her deceased brother, or pick up the phone so that she can read it to him.

This form of denial will cease when bereaved persons have fully accepted the reality of their loved one's death. After that, whenever they see a certain newspaper article, or a certain pair of shoes, they will still think that their loved one would have enjoyed reading the article or wearing the shoes. But this type of thinking is not a form of denial. They are not forgetting that their loved one is dead. They are remembering that he or she once lived.

FEAR

Shortly after the death, persons in grief begin to feel fear. They know that their lives have permanently changed in negative ways that are both tangible and intangible. They are afraid of these changes and question their ability to cope with them.

A young mother stands at her husband's grave holding hands with her son and daughter. When the service is over she walks away wondering if she is capable of being both mother and father to her children. Will she have the energy to keep up with their activities, her career, and maintaining her home? When her husband was alive they solved any problems they had by discussing them together. With him gone will she have the strength and know-how to solve similar problems by herself?

An elderly man sits alone in his house the day after his wife's funeral. He knows he can learn to do the grocery shopping, the cooking, the cleaning, and the laundry. But who will give him companionship and love? Who will laugh at his jokes and admire the bouquets of flowers he gathers from the garden he tends to so diligently? Who will share the morning newspaper with him, an afternoon cup of coffee, or a night of watching television?

The young woman fears being alone. The elderly man fears being lonely. For a very long time, because they will continue to discover negative ways in which the deaths of their loved ones have altered their lives, their fear will worsen. And no one, not even another bereaved person, will be able to reason or to cajole them out of being afraid.

As grieving individuals move farther into the grieving process and encounter more and more of the emotions of grief, additional fears can develop. Never before have they felt such a variety of painful emotions simultaneously. Attempting to deal with this glut of emotion makes it nearly impossible for them to concentrate on anything but their grief.

As their inability to concentrate worsens, they become forgetful and confused.

Two months after my daughter died, I was confronted with the task of preparing for Christmas. Prior to her death, this had been my favorite holiday, and I willingly put a great deal of effort into making it special. That year, of course, the thought of celebrating what had always been a happy occasion, only heightened my realization that I was bitterly unhappy. But, because I treasured the traditions I shared with my family and friends, I forced myself into a state of mind resembling the holiday spirit. A week or so before December 25th, when I began wrapping gifts, I was shocked to see that I had made duplicate purchases. I had two of this gift, and two of that gift, and even worse, I could not remember buying any of them. My forgetfulness caused me to become depressed. As I had always associated depression with mental illness, I wondered if I was going insane. The very thought of insanity terrified me. Much later, after speaking with other bereaved persons, I learned that depression is a normal reaction to a significant loss, and my fear began to subside. But, to this day, I can remember the terror I felt and how unpleasant it was.

After the death of their loved one, bereaved persons spiral downward into a black hole filled with painful and frightening emotions. These emotions cause them to feel so bad, they begin to doubt that they will ever feel good again. They know that the quality of their lives is extremely poor and they fear that it will never improve. In this debilitated state, they also fear that they will not be able to cope with their grief or find ways to work through it.

During the grieving process, all people experience one or more fears. The number and variety depend on their emotional make-up as well as their status in life before and after the death. These same factors will determine, in part, the length of the grieving process.

GUILT

I once asked a bereavement support group facilitator if she knew the reason why most bereaved persons feel guilty after a loved one dies. "No, I don't," the facilitator answered. "But most of them do express feelings of guilt. They seem to think that they should have done something to prevent the death."

If the loved one who dies is very old, those mourning the death can easily understand why death occurred. This does not make their grief any easier to bear, but it can make the death easier to accept.

If the deceased is a child, a teenager, or a young or middle-aged adult, the reaction is quite different. Even though those mourning the death know the cause of death, they struggle to understand why—out of all the people in the world—their child, or their wife, or their husband, for example, was the one who had to die. They tell themselves there must be a reason for the death, and they need to know that reason. Was it something they did or did not do? Could they have prevented the death? They begin to believe they failed their loved one in some way. They are ashamed of their failure and they begin to feel guilt.

The shame felt by grieving individuals causes them to be reluctant to discuss their guilt with anyone other than another person in grief or members of a bereavement support group. During such discussions all parties involved will preface their statements with, "I should have . . ." or "I should not have . . ."

For instance, during a sharing session for grieving spouses, a wife might say that she should have stopped her husband from eating snacks high in saturated fat and drinking beer while he was watching television. A husband will respond by saying that he understands how the grieving wife feels because even though he suspected that his wife was ill, he did not make her see a doctor. Or, during a sharing session for grieving parents, a father might say that he should not have bought his son a car for his sixteenth birthday. A mother will respond by saying that she understands how the grieving father feels because she should not have allowed her daughter to swim in a neighbor's pool unless she was there to watch her.

In the beginning of grief, it makes no difference to the grieving wife and the grieving husband that they could not control their spouses' behavior. It makes no difference to the grieving father and the grieving mother that children have fatal accidents no matter how hard parents try to prevent them. They don't understand that something they did or did not do was not the cause of the death. And that they have no valid reason to feel guilty. They do not understand that guilt is a product of their struggle to ascertain why their loved one, a person who was good, had died rather than some other person who was not so good.

Chance comments made by others can also cause those in grief to feel guilt. For instance, if the grieving father described above overhears someone say, "Sixteen-year-olds are irresponsible and should not be given driver's licenses." or "Most teenagers drive like maniacs." he might think the person making the comment is implying that he is to blame for his son's death. He should not have allowed his son to obtain a driver's license. Or he should have taught his son the safe and proper way to drive a car. At this point in time, the father is so immersed in his grief, he is unable to reason that he is no different from the thousands of other parents who allow their children to drive cars at age sixteen. And that any one of these children could be killed in an accident.

It is sometimes difficult for us to comprehend the guilt that often accompanies grief. Like denial, it seems to be another form of irrational and illogical thinking. As bereaved persons begin to heal, they too will see that they have no reason to be guilty. In the meantime, they see their guilt as a reality rather than a product of their need to know why their loved one died.

ANGER

Anger is one of the most complex emotions of grief. It is also the one that weighs most heavily on grieving individuals. From its root cause, the death, it branches out in many directions. Each branch is a separate reason to be angry.

Initially, people in grief can be angry with the deceased. Without this person, they are lost and alone. As implausible as it might sound, they can feel that their loved one abandoned them. A sense of abandonment is more prevalent in some types of grief than it is in others. Two that immediately come to mind are the deaths of a spouse and of a parent.

The young husband whose wife dies will miss being involved in his wife's life, and he will miss her being involved in his. He will miss being loved, and he will miss having her to love. He will be angry that her death created a void in his life. If the couple had children, the young husband will soon discover that rearing them alone is not as easy as it appears to be on television or in the movies. He can be angry with her for leaving him with such an exacting and frightening responsibility. If the couple was childless, the young husband can be angry that they did not have a child. He thinks that a child would help fill the void in his life, and that he would still have someone special to love.

Spouses in other age groups also feel anger. A middle-aged wife can be angry with her husband because, after years of working, scrimping, and saving, he died before they had a chance to retire and enjoy a life of leisure. An elderly husband coping with health problems can be angry with his wife for deserting him when he needed her the most.

If the spouse committed suicide, developed a fatal illness that might have been prevented, or indulged in life-threatening activities, the surviving spouse's anger can be intensified. In some cases, it is so intense it will never completely dissipate.

The young husband, the middle-aged wife, and the elderly husband are not being selfish or self-centered. By nature, most of us are optimists. We live our lives expecting good things to happen to us. We expect the people we love to be there for us. When things don't work out the way we thought they would, we feel betrayed. Our natural reaction to betrayal is anger.

Children who lose a parent also feel abandoned. The permanent changes that occur in their lives can be much more devastating than the changes that occur in the lives of bereaved adults. If the surviving parent is forced to sell the family home the children will be moved to a new neighborhood and a new school. Everything that is familiar to them will be taken away. Many children, especially young ones, have a very hard time understanding the changes taking place in their lives and why these changes are necessary.

Because children are unable to take care of themselves, and are dependent on their parents, the death of one parent leaves them vulnerable. They miss the security of having two parents. They become angry with the parent who died, and with the surviving parent who, due to his or her own grief, might not be fully aware of the child's insecurity.

It can be extremely difficult for bereaved persons to admit that they are angry with the loved one who left them. Had the deceased been able to choose life over death, surely he or she would have chosen life. And so they often direct their anger toward the medical personnel who were unable to save their loved one's life. Or, if the death was the result of an accident, their anger is directed toward the person who caused the accident.

While people in grief are experiencing feelings of guilt, they can be angry with themselves. Had they done this . . . had they not done that . . . their loved one might still be alive. Why hadn't they tried harder to lift their loved one's depression, enforced better health habits, or spoken out against the life-threatening activity?

If they are religious, they can be angry with God as well. In their prayers they asked that He protect their loved one, and He did not. They lost their loved one and, for a while, they can lose their faith in God. This double loss can greatly increase their anger and their suffering.

In order to recover from grief, bereaved persons must voice their anger. If they are ashamed to do so, or have no one who is willing to listen to them without passing judgment, they can express their anger in inappropriate ways. For example, a grieving wife can berate a department store salesperson for not being able to locate a blouse she wants to buy in a certain size and color. Or a grieving father can become irate with a cashier in a grocery store because the scanner did not ring up the sale price of an item. The salesperson and the cashier are innocent victims of the bottled-up anger churning inside the wife and the father. Neither understands why they were treated harshly, and both are hurt and bewildered.

The wife and the father might also be bewildered as to why they became irate. Prior to the death of the wife's husband, and the death of the father's child, such minor incidents did not cause them to react so strongly. The force of their anger frightens them, and they attempt to pinpoint its source. As they move forward in the grieving process, they become stronger. Eventually, they will be able to admit to themselves that they are angry because they feel lost and alone, or even abandoned. They will see the need to express their anger in constructive ways, and, if they truly want to resolve their grief, they will turn to a family member or friend for help, join a bereavement support group, or seek the counsel of a grief specialist.

RESENTFULNESS

At the same time people in grief are struggling to cope with their guilt and anger, they begin to feel the stirrings of resentfulness. Like anger, resentfulness branches out in many directions and can be aimed at anyone with whom they come in contact, as well as situations they encounter.

The death of their loved one forced them out of a world that was happy and safe and into one filled with anguish and fear. It takes time for them to adjust to being banished from their old world and to find a place in the new one.

While they are striving to accustom themselves to their new world, their friends, neighbors, and co-workers continue to enjoy life in the old one. Unaware that bereaved persons feel displaced and alienated, the friends, neighbors, and co-workers are also unaware that their enjoyment is tormenting the grieving person.

A young woman grieves the death of her dearest friend. The two women met when they were children and have been constant companions ever since. When her friend died, the young woman's life was traumatically altered. Internally, she now asks several questions: Why can't the people around her see how sad and lonely she is? Why aren't they devoting themselves to helping her overcome her grief? How can they continue to be happy and to carry on with their lives when she is so miserable? How can they continue to joke and to laugh in her presence? If the young woman asked these questions out loud, family members, friends, and co-workers would respond that they cannot be expected to put their lives on hold until the young woman recovers from her grief. This is, of course, true, and the young woman subconsciously knows it. However, she cannot help resenting those who live in the old world. She does not resent the happiness they share with their families and friends. But the happiness she sees all around her reminds her that she, too, once had an enjoyable life. She resents that she will never have that same life again.

Resentfulness locks grieving individuals into a catch-22 situation. On one hand, they dread associating with people who are not experiencing grief because it places them in situations that point out the grim ways in which their lives have changed. On the other hand, they must continue to associate with these people or run the risk of losing the support and companionship they offer. They do not want to wake up one day and find themselves completely alone.

When bereaved persons are at home, they are surrounded by remnants of their loved ones' lives. A grieving husband finds an old coat that belonged to his wife hanging on the back of the basement door. As his hand touches the coat, the smell of her perfume wafts out at him, and he remembers the joy she brought to his life. A grieving grandson stares at the picture of his deceased grandmother sitting atop his desk. He remembers her teaching him to play Chinese Checkers when he was a child, and how delighted she was whenever he won. A grieving mother stands beside her deceased son's crib spinning the mobile that hangs overhead. She remembers how wonderful it was when he smiled up at her, and how proud she was when he rolled over for the very first time.

Venturing into the outside world is no better. In the grocery store, the grieving husband sees loving couples shopping together. While jogging in the park the grieving grandson encounters grandmothers and their grandchildren playing together. When the grieving mother goes to the shopping mall, she watches other young mothers pushing their babies in strollers. Each of these three is reminded of what they have lost, and their hearts shatter anew.

I do not want you to confuse resentfulness with envy. Bereaved individuals do not envy the relationships other people share with their own loved ones. They would not wish the agony and anguish of a lost relationship on any other person. But they are resentful. The death of their loved one removed them from the comfort of their old world. They resent having to live in their new world of grief.

Grieving individuals can also resent people who neglect, or even abuse, members of their own families, as well as those who do not nurture the relationships they share with others. They cannot understand why these people ignore, or mistreat, something so precious. They resent having lost future opportunities to be with their loved one while others, who still have those opportunities, choose to toss them aside.

In some cases, they also resent the life-altering situations the death created. If it was preceded by a lengthy, and very costly illness, they might have been left with a mountain of unpaid bills. They do not resent being in debt. They would willingly go into debt again. But they do resent that their loved one died in spite of it. In other cases, bereaved persons are elderly couples who, after the death of their adult child, must assume the responsibility of rearing their grandchildren. They do not resent their grandchildren's presence in their lives, but they do resent having to take on a responsibility that, because of their age, they are not sure they are capable of handling. Those who are struggling to cope with additional problems, such as being in debt or having their grandchildren come live with them, cannot concentrate on recovering from their grief. They have more immediate issues to deal with. Until these issues are resolved, recovery will be delayed, and they will be in pain for a longer period of time. This, in itself, is another reason for them to be resentful.

Helplessness

When we were children, adults controlled our lives and made most of our decisions for us. At times, we attempted to change those decisions and, when we could not, we felt helpless. We vowed that when we grew up, we would be in control. We would never feel helpless again.

Many persons in grief feel as helpless as they did when they were children because they could not prevent their loved one's death. They are frustrated that, once again, they are not able to control events occurring in their lives. This combination of helplessness and frustration can be quite devastating.

If death occurred after an illness, some bereaved individuals, even though they watched their loved one move closer and closer to death during the illness, continued to hope for a complete recovery. Along with that hope, came the desire to transfer some of their strength to their loved one. They willed their loved one to live. Attempting to transfer their strength, and to will recovery, gave them a sense of being helpful rather than helpless. When their loved one died they were hit hard with the knowledge that their efforts were useless. This knowledge enhances the helplessness they feel after the death.

If death occurred suddenly, some grieving individuals experience the same feeling of helplessness. And it can be tinged with imagined guilt. Should the grieving wife have been able to predict and prevent the heart attack that killed her husband? Should the grieving parents have been able to predict and prevent the accident that killed their child? Until the grieving wife and the grieving parents come to the realization that no one can accurately predict the future, and that all of us, although we make mistakes, do the best we can on any given day, they yearn to return to the time when their loved ones were alive. But this is not possible. They are powerless to change the past, and have no choice but to learn to live in the present.

Learning to live in the present is a long and painful process. In the beginning of that process, it can be impossible for people in grief to control their emotions. Wherever they go, or whatever they do, a sound, a sight, or a smell will remind them of their loved one's death.

A week or so after his mother's funeral, a grieving son turns on the car radio and hears her favorite song. Later that same day, he drives by the place where she worked. Although he has not cried since he was a boy, after each of these incidents, he breaks down and cries uncontrollably. Several months later, when he is still breaking down after encountering similar reminders, he realizes that he is powerless to control his emotions. When the pain caused by his mother's absence from his life engulfs him, he has no choice but to succumb.

It is very disconcerting for bereaved persons not to be able to control their emotions. When they cry in public, they are embarrassed, and the people around them are uncomfortable. Crying in the privacy of their homes is a bit better, but still they feel helplessly out of control. Eventually, they become even more frustrated; when will they regain the ability to govern their emotions?

As bereaved individuals work through the grieving process, reminders of their loved one become less painful, and they break down less often. On occasion their emotions still get the best of them, but overall, they are back in control. Their feeling of helplessness subsides.

At this point, those who are experiencing grief for the first time can mistakenly believe that, because they are back in control and no longer feel helpless, their grief is coming to an end. They do not know that the road to recovery can be long and rocky. These people, especially if they have lost someone to whom they were extremely close, soon discover that their agony, although it is not as close to the surface as it was in the beginning, still churns inside them. They yearn to be as happy as they once were, but their ongoing grief makes this impossible. A feeling of helplessness again washes over them. They have been in pain for such a long time and, no matter what they do or how hard they work to resolve their grief, they seem incapable of doing so.

Grief is not a predictable process in either form or duration. The accompanying pain ebbs and flows. On a day when the pain has eased, bereaved persons can believe they have recovered. The next day, when a reminder of their loved one brings back the pain, they know they have not. Some begin to wonder if they will ever recover.

Until they realize that each person's grief is unique, and that it can last for months or years, they will feel helpless.

DETACHMENT

As explained previously, the death of a loved one causes persons in grief to feel alienated from their old world. Linked to this alienation is a sense of being detached or disconnected from those who still live in that world. In a manner of speaking, they have walked through an invisible door. When the door closed behind them, it shut off the life they once knew, and they found themselves face-to-face with the grieving process. While in grief they have but one reality: Their loved one's death has left them bereft, frightened, and in pain.

Prior to the death, their reality was quite different. They were secure with themselves, and they fit snugly into their environment. They were interested in world, national, and local issues because these issues had the potential to impact on their lives. They questioned whether or not these issues would eventually affect them: Would their son or daughter someday be transported overseas to defend a nation incapable of defending itself? Would their state government increase property taxes and cause them financial hardship? Would their neighborhoods become unsafe? Events occurring in the lives of their families and friends also impacted their lives. Sharing in the celebration of weddings, births, and other joyous occasions made them happy. And, when misfortune struck in the life of someone to whom they were close, they willingly offered to help. The world they lived in before the death was, for the most part, comfortable and satisfying, vast and wide.

After the death, their world narrows down to one of pain and mourning. Trapped within the confines of grief, they struggle to recover. Due to their need to recover, they devote their time and energy to that struggle and limit their interest in events occurring within the world, the community, and their families.

To those who have not experienced death-loss grief, the limits bereaved persons place on their interest in world and local affairs, and in the lives of their family and friends, might appear to be a deliberate attempt to disconnect from anything that does not pertain to their bereavement. But this is not true. They do not deliberately disconnect from the people around them for two reasons. First, like displaced persons yearning to return to the familiarity of their place of birth, they yearn to return to the familiarity of the world they inhabited prior to the death. Second, they realize that if they are going to conquer their grief, they need the support of family members and friends. And so they strive to remain connected.

In the beginning of grief, staying connected is almost impossible. Bereaved persons are saturated with their pain and with the void the death of their loved one created in their lives. They have trouble concentrating on anything else.

The wife who mourns the death of her husband has no interest in baking his favorite cake. Grieving parents see no reason to check the status of their deceased child's college fund. Conversations with co-workers or friends that a grieving husband once found stimulating, now seem trite and mundane. If attempts are made to involve them in these or similar activities, they will show little interest. If pressured to participate they might even go into seclusion.

This lack of concentration and inability to focus presents itself to the outside world as absent-mindedness or forgetfulness. During this period of time it is difficult for anyone to interact with the person in grief. It is never easy for one person to converse with another person whose thoughts are focused elsewhere.

If people begin to avoid them because they are forgetful and absent-minded their grief is compounded. They are already feeling detached from the world around them; they are already lonely for the person who died. Being avoided by their family and friends increases their loneliness.

MEANINGLESSNESS

In order for us to thrive and grow, both mentally and emotionally, our lives must have purpose and meaning. We give our lives meaning by functioning in ways that satisfy ourselves as well as the people we love.

Satisfying ourselves might mean devoting time to a leisure activity that brings us pleasure, or doing some type of volunteer work that we find fulfilling. Although our loved ones might not physically participate in these activities with us, we do share these activities with them by telling them of our accomplishments.

Satisfying the people we love can mean devoting time to making the lives of our family members more pleasant and worthwhile. For example, a wife will put in extra hours at work with the intent of using the additional income she earns to surprise her husband with a luxurious cruise on their twenty-fifth wedding anniversary. Or a mother and father will devote their spare time to attending school functions and other events in which their child is involved. If the husband dies before his wife can give him the cruise, or if the child dies, a physical void is left in the lives of the wife and of the parents. Prior to the death, most of their spare hours were filled with activity relating to their husband and to their child. What they achieved during those hours, as wife and as parents, gave their lives purpose and meaning. After the deaths there is no reason for them to function as they once did. For a while, because they have lost their reason to function, they can view their lives as empty and meaningless.

The death of a loved one also leaves an emotional void in the lives of grieving individuals. While the deceased was alive, they gave of themselves to him or to her; they offered love and support and reaped the benefits of having love and support returned to them. They were there when their loved one needed them. And their loved one was there for them. After the death they continue to love the deceased. This love can be expressed by visiting the grave, by keeping it tidy and covered with flowers. But, because these expressions of love cannot compare to the love expressed by a hug, a kiss, or a conversation, they do not mean the same. They are not as fulfilling and satisfying. They can even seem hollow and meaningless.

Hopefully, no adult has just one reason for living. But in many cases, the main, or most important reason does center around a family member, a lover, a friend, or someone we care about deeply.

Let's go back to the bereaved wife and the bereaved parents discussed previously. The wife spent a great deal of time with her husband. In concert, they worked toward the common goal of making their life together gratifying and complete. The relationship between the grieving parents and their deceased child was demanding and time consuming. The parents were required to provide for their child's physical needs and to prepare him or her, both intellectually and emotionally, to enter adulthood.

The wife and the parents both had a mission in life. Although these missions were quite different, they were of equal importance. When the deaths occurred these missions were aborted. For some time after the deaths, the wife and the parents will see little reason to get out of bed in the morning. The hours that once were filled to capacity with physically and emotionally nurturing the relationships they treasured, now stretch out before them—long and empty. Eventually they will find new missions in life, and new ways to fill their vacant hours. But, until they do, their lives will seem meaningless.

* * *

During the grieving process, bereaved persons can be plagued by all of the nine core emotions of grief.

With the exception of shock, which is normally felt immediately after the death of their loved one, there is no set pattern for when they will experience these emotions. There will be times when only one emotion is felt. There will be times when several are felt simultaneously. There will be times when the grieving individuals flip-flop back and forth between emotions. There will also be times when an emotion disappears only to reappear a few months or a few years later. The fact that grief emotions appear, disappear, and then reappear frightens them, and causes them to wonder if they are ever going to recover.

It also points out why grief is such a complex process, and why it is so important for those who are attempting to interact with bereaved persons to gain a thorough understanding of that process. This can best be accomplished by encouraging the grieving individual to share his or her true feelings with you. You can also talk with persons who have experienced the same type of grief as the individual with whom you are attempting to interact or with bereavement support group facilitators, and by reading books written about specific types of grief. An easy way to determine what books have been published, as well as what books are soon to be published, is to contact the librarian who mans the information desk in your local library.

CHAPTER 2

Factors That Can Affect Grief

Last night our quiet neighborhood became a nightmare! In a house on the next street over a boy beat his father with a baseball bat. You talk about bringing our son's murder back to us. Even the temperature was the same as the night we heard about our boy.

Melanie
9-5-95

The death of a loved one is a tragic event—an event that permanently alters our lives—an event that we grieve.

During the grieving process we experience a variety of painful emotions. But experiencing these emotions is not all there is to grief. Often, due to internal or external factors, our response to grief can be heightened or diminished. The pain we feel can be excruciating and last for a very long time, or it can be brief and relatively mild.

Internal factors can, for example, include our personalities or how we felt about the deceased, despite his or her relationship to us. External factors can include events that occurred in the past, that are occurring at the time of the death, or that will occur shortly thereafter. Usually, we have no control over these factors. Our personalities are already formed. They make us the one-of-a-kind individuals we are. And we do not orchestrate many of the events that occur in our lives. They happen whether we want them to or not.

As you know there is no right or wrong way to grieve. This is due, in part, to internal and external factors that are unique to each of us and to our individual lives. The reasons we grieve in a specific way are sometimes known only to us. Although we understand these reasons, there are times when those witnessing our grief do not. Because these people do not understand, they might become concerned that how we are grieving is a deviation from what they consider to be normal. Although they do not mean to harm us, if they attempt to interfere with our grief, we can be hurt.

Following is a sampling of some of the factors that can impact the way in which bereaved persons grieve. After reading them you will have a better understanding of why grief is such a diverse and highly personal process, and why it is so complex.

FACTOR NO. 1 THE ROLE THE DECEASED PLAYED IN THE LIFE OF THE BEREAVED PERSON

If you are an employee of a large company or corporation, you have probably been given a personnel manual that describes, in great detail, company policy. In that manual is a section on what is sometimes called "death leave."

More than likely, under that death leave policy, you, as an employee, will be given more time off from work when your spouse, parent, child, grandchild, brother, or sister dies than when your aunt, uncle, niece, nephew, grandparent, brother-in-law, or sister-in-law dies. When formulating the "death leave" policy, your company's administrators arbitrarily assumed that certain family members are more important in your life than are others. In many cases this assumption is correct. In some, it is not.

During the late seventies and early eighties I was the Personnel Manager of a mid-size manufacturing company. One morning a young female employee came to me with the news that her uncle had died. "According to the Personnel Manual," she said, "I can only be excused from work for one day. But one day is not enough time. I need more."

I could see that this woman was very distraught. Her eyes were red rimmed and puffy from crying, and in one trembling hand, she clenched the shredded remains of a soggy tissue. I asked her to sit down and tell me a little about her uncle. It turned out that her father was a workaholic who had always devoted the bulk of his time to his career rather than to his daughter. Because of this, her uncle had stepped in and assumed the role of father. He had taken her to museums, the movies, and the zoo. He had taught her to garden, and to drive a car. Over the years, she had bonded with her uncle in a way that she had not bonded with her father. Although she loved her father, his presence in her life had not been as important to her as her uncle's. Now that he was dead, her life would be less joyous and, at times, very lonely.

Because of the close relationship the young woman had shared with her uncle, she felt she needed several days away from work. She wanted to help her aunt make the funeral arrangements which, she hoped, would include four viewings and a small gathering of friends after the burial. She also felt that she needed some time alone to accept the reality of her uncle's death and to say goodbye.

In many cases it is difficult to know the role the deceased played in the lives of bereaved persons or the type of relationship they shared. Assumptions cannot be made that certain individuals are not deeply affected by the death. If assumptions are made, limits are placed on their grief. These limits are detrimental in that they do not allow the time and atmosphere necessary for the full expression of grief.

Before I leave this factor and move on to the next I want to add a footnote to the employee's story.

After we had worked out a way for her to take the time off from work she needed, she thanked me graciously and left my office. Sitting alone, thinking about her situation, I wondered how she would react when her father died. Would she feel guilty that her uncle's presence in her life had meant more to her than her father's? Would she go through a period of wishing that she had demanded her fair share of her father's time?

Logically, there was no reason why this woman should feel guilty. She was not to blame for her father's failure to take an active interest in her life. It is impossible for children to control the behavior of adults, including that of their parents.

But grief is not a logical process. It is a process comprised of painful emotions necessary to the resolution of grief. One of these emotions can be guilt. In the majority of cases there is no valid reason for grieving individuals to feel guilty. But still they do—perhaps for no reason other than that they are still alive, enjoying life, and their loved one is dead.

It is important for grieving individuals, and all who interact with them either personally or professionally, to know that imagined guilts can enhance grief and lengthen the period of mourning.

FACTOR NO. 2
HOW THE DEATH ALTERS THE LIFE OF THE BEREAVED PERSON

Eight years after my daughter died, the husband of one of my friends was killed in a car accident.

My friend had married her husband when they were both eighteen years old. After the marriage, he had joined the military, and eventually, had made it his career. Most of their life together had been spent overseas. Toward the end of his career, he was assigned to a base in Maryland. Two years later, when he retired from the military, the couple considered moving back to their home state. But because their daughter was still in high school, they did not want to uproot her. They built a beautiful new house near their daughter's school and prepared to settle down. At the time of the fatal car accident, they had been living in their home for less than a month.

On a warm spring evening, two years after my friend's husband was killed, she and I were strolling through a small park near her home. To our right was a bank of azaleas, their magenta blossoms glowing warmly in the setting sun. To our left, young couples romped with their children on jungle gyms and swings set up in a fence-enclosed play area. The sight of these people having such a good time made me think about how much I missed my daughter, and the many ways in which her death had altered my life. And I knew that my friend was thinking the same about her husband and his death.

With a smile on her face, my friend told me that her marriage had been wonderful. "Not only did I love my husband with my whole heart," she said, "but he was also my best friend. I was with him for so long I can't imagine dating another man—even though I hate having to go everywhere alone."

Then, no longer smiling, she said that she was hard pressed to keep up with the responsibilities of working a full-time job and trying to maintain her home and property by herself. "I don't have the physical strength to do some of the maintenance," she told me, "and I can't find a contractor who just wants to do odd jobs. My husband's family and mine both live out of state, and I don't like asking my neighbors for help.

"I know it was horrible for you when your daughter died," she continued. "But at least you weren't all alone. You still had your husband to go places with and to do the heavy work around the house."

Later that night I thought about what my friend had said. Her husband's death had adversely affected her life in many ways. And she was right. I was glad that I still had my husband to help me. I was glad that I was not all alone.

When a death occurs, permanent, negative changes are made in the lives of those who mourn the death. While they are struggling to adjust to these changes, their grief is disrupted. It's hard to keep one's mind on the grieving process while coping with problems caused by the death. These problems can complicate grief and can make it harder to bear.

FACTOR NO. 3
THE STATUS OF THE BEREAVED PERSON'S LIFE AT THE TIME OF THE DEATH

Today, you are not exactly the same person you were ten years ago. And ten years from now you will have changed again. For instance, the problems you will be dealing with in your everyday life might be easier or more difficult for you to handle. Your health might have gone from good to poor or vice versa. You might have more free time, and more money to spend, or you might have less of both. Whatever the future holds in store for you it will make you a different person from the person you are now.

The other day, while eating lunch in the restaurant area of a shopping mall, I overheard two women seated at a nearby table discussing the funeral of a mutual friend's mother. Both of these women appeared to be in their early sixties. Each was surrounded by packages. The mall was pulsating with life and color. Shoppers of all ages streamed past my table. Multi-hued banners hung from wires attached to the ceiling. As I listened to what the women were saying, I thought that the mall—a place filled with life—was a strange place to be having a conversation about death. And because I wondered what had triggered their conversation, I moved my chair closer to their table and listened more intently.

In the past, both women had suffered the deaths of their parents. Even though they had both experienced the same type of grief, that of losing their mother and father, each had responded to the death of each parent differently.

"When my father died, my children were in elementary school," said one of the women. "I didn't see him very often. He worked during the week and, on weekends, I was busy with my husband, my children, and all of their activities. Neither I nor my mother worked, so we had time to do things together while my children were in school.

"After my father died, my mother spent a lot of time at my house. And eventually she moved in with us. Over the years she and I became very close. Because I was not as close to my father as I was to my mother, I didn't grieve as intensely when he died as I did when she died. And I didn't grieve nearly as long."

The other woman thought a moment and then said, "It's hard for me to compare what I felt when my mom died to what I felt when my dad died. When my mom died I was in the process of getting a divorce, and I was working two full-time jobs just to keep my head above water. My kids were terribly upset by their father leaving them, and so was I. I was exhausted and never had a minute to call my own. My mom's death was just one more disaster in my disastrous life. I was so overwhelmed I couldn't even cry. People must have thought that her death didn't matter to me. But it did.

"When my dad died my life was better and less hectic. I had fewer problems and I wasn't as distracted. I felt the full impact of his death the minute I heard the news, and was so sad, the tears poured out of me. I guess, because I cried at my dad's funeral but not at my mom's, people thought I loved him more than I did her."

The ways in which bereaved individuals grieve can be determined by events occurring in their lives at the time of the death. The trauma caused by these events might be so disturbing and so overwhelming it detracts from the trauma caused by the death. The depth of a bereaved person's grief cannot be assessed by external displays of emotion.

FACTOR NO. 4
PAST EXPERIENCES IN THE BEREAVED PERSON'S LIFE

After my daughter's death, I became a member of a support group for bereaved parents. Although I did not attend meetings on a regular basis, I often spoke with other members of the group by phone. I will never forget one of the mothers I spoke with frequently.

The woman's son had died in a car accident. In the beginning of her grief, although her voice was heavy with pain and sorrow when she spoke with me, it did, on occasion, spark with life. There was even a time or two when she laughed at some silly joke I made. As time passed, she stopped laughing all together, and her voice sounded as if it were dead. She told me that she had stopped eating, and that even though she was tired all the time, she could not sleep. It was apparent that she had become despondent and deeply depressed.

At first I attributed her worsening state to her emergence from shock. Without shock to protect her from the painful emotions she was feeling, she was fully experiencing her grief for the very first time. I tried to console her, and to lift her spirits. But despite my efforts, she sank deeper into despair to the point where she threatened to take her life.

I knew what it was like to lose a child, and that despair and despondency are normal reactions to child-death grief. Although I had no right to judge this woman, I began to think that her grief was excessive and out of the ordinary. Then I reasoned that there might be another reason why she was grieving so deeply. Ever so gently, I started probing into her background.

After several unsuccessful attempts to uncover the cause of her worsening grief, I finally managed to ask the right question: "In the past did you suffer any other significant death?"

The woman began to sob. "Yes," she answered. "My first husband, my son's real father, died when my son was two years old."

Until then I had no idea that the man to whom this woman was married was not her first husband, or that he was her son's stepfather.

The woman continued. "I married my second husband ten months after my first husband died," she said. "I guess I married again too quickly. I didn't give myself time to mourn my first husband's death. When my son was killed in the accident it brought my husband's death back to me. It seems like I am now grieving for him and for my son."

It is sometimes impossible to know the complete history of grieving individuals, or how that history affects the intensity of their grief. Tragedies that occurred in the past can complicate the grieving process and can cause a bereaved person's grief to seem excessive when, because of his or her history, it is not.

FACTOR NO. 5
TRAUMAS SUFFERED IN THE PAST BY OTHER MEMBERS OF THE BEREAVED PERSON'S FAMILY

On occasion I speak at a meeting of a homicide bereavement support group. Prior to each meeting, as the room fills with people, the air becomes thick with the tension of those who have come to share their grief. At the same time, in the back of the room, a coffeepot bubbles merrily. But the people in the room are oblivious to the bubbling song the coffeepot sings, and the rich aroma the brewing liquid sends into the air.

During the meeting the tension increases. Tears are shed and stories of horror are told. But afterward, when it is over, the tension begins to subside. Those in attendance pour themselves a cup of coffee and mill about talking with people they have met before and introducing themselves to people who are new to the group.

Recently, at one of these meetings, I spoke with a woman whose daughter had been murdered twelve years ago. After the murder, the family had gone through a terrible period of pain and suffering. Even though this woman knew that she would never fully recover from her daughter's murder and never be completely free from pain, she had finally come to accept it.

"The worst of my grief is behind me," she told me. But the pain evident in her eyes and in her voice did not match the optimism of her words. It seemed to me that something had rekindled her grief.

Farther along in our conversation, I learned that the woman's niece had committed suicide the year before. My initial reaction was one of shock and sorrow. How, I wondered, could her family manage to survive two such terrible tragedies? When my shock began to subside, I asked the woman, "How did your niece's death make you feel?"

"I was, of course, filled with pain," she answered. "Her suicide was, as they say, a permanent solution to a temporary problem. I was sorry that she had chosen to end her life rather than to ask for our help. And I knew that I would miss her for the rest of my life just as I will miss my daughter. For a while, my niece's death brought the memory of my daughter's death back to me in full force."

"But that was only half of it. I also knew the agony my sister was going to suffer. I knew she was going to feel anger, despair, and even more painful emotions. I wanted desperately to spare her the same kind of suffering I had endured when my daughter died, but I knew I could not. Knowing that I could not, increased my pain. I still feel horrible about it."

Traumas suffered by members of bereaved persons' families can rekindle the powerful emotions they felt at the height of their initial grief. When it appears that they have been thrown back to square one, or have switched from progression to regression, it is necessary to carefully dig beneath the surface to uncover the cause of the regression.

FACTOR NO. 6 WHO REMAINS IN THE BEREAVED PERSON'S LIFE AFTER THE DEATH

Every once in a while several of my female friends and I get together for an all-night gab fest. Each woman brings a snack or an exotic beverage to share with the group. And, to ensure that we never get stuck in a conversational rut, each is encouraged to invite a woman the group has never met.

During one of these gab fests, after we had cured the ills of the world and solved all of its problems, we somehow got on the subject of grief. One of our invited guests told the group that her mother, who had been a widow for fourteen years, had recently died.

As personal representative of her mother's estate, it was this woman's responsibility to ensure that the terms of her mother's will were carried out to the letter. Because she and her two younger sisters were to share equally in the estate and, more importantly, because their mother's death was a trauma that required a joint effort to survive, she had asked her sisters to accompany her when she went to the bank to empty out the safe deposit box, and to the courthouse to file the will.

"In the bank," she said, "while waiting for the manager to finish a transaction he was working on with another customer, my sisters and I sat, like three ducks in a row, on a bench outside the manager's office. Suddenly, one of my sisters looked at me and said, 'I just had the most horrible thought. Now that Mom is dead, we three are orphans.'"

"At first," the woman continued, "because it seemed outlandish to think of women in their forties and fifties as orphans, I thought my sister was making a joke to lighten our situation. But then I realized her statement was true. Despite our advanced ages we were, to all intents and purposes, orphans."

"Later that day, my sisters and I discussed, in depth, our new status in life. And we agreed it was somewhat frightening. In the past, no matter that we were mature adults, we could go to our mother for help and advice at any time. Now that she was dead, we were the senior females in our individual families. Our children and grandchildren could come to us for advice, but to whom could we go?"

"That day I looked at my grief from a new perspective. I sagged under the weight of the responsibility of being the senior female in the family. And my sister's statement gave me another reason to miss my mother."

A wide range of elements can effect the way in which bereaved persons grieve, and can change the weight and meaning of their grief. So it is always wise, when interacting with someone whose grief might seem to be out of proportion to the death suffered, to look at the situation from another angle.

FACTOR NO. 7
THE PERSONALITY OF THE BEREAVED PERSON

Who among us has not heard the expression, "One person's trash is another person's treasure." This old saying can be interpreted in many different ways. One interpretation is that one person's likes and dislikes can differ radically from those of another simply because each person has a unique personality unlike that of any other person.

Shortly before I began doing research for this book, I attended the funeral of the brother of a friend of mine. After the funeral, the mourners met in a room in the church of which the brother was a member for a light lunch hosted by my friend. While I was filling my plate at the buffet table, the elderly woman standing next to me whispered in my direction, "I don't understand our hostess. I haven't seen her shed one tear over the death of her brother. Why, when my brother died back in '72, I cried so many tears I could have filled an ocean. What's wrong with her? Didn't she love her brother?"

I knew that my friend loved her brother very much and that they had shared a close relationship. I also knew that my friend was a private and reserved person. She, too, would shed many tears over her brother's death. But her tears would be shed only when she was by herself.

For a moment I debated telling the elderly woman why my friend was not crying openly. Instead, I commented that the fruit salad smelled delicious and recommended that she try a spoonful or two.

Obviously this elderly woman had a relaxed and easy-going personality. She carried her emotions close to the surface and expressed her opinions freely. Because free expression was part of her personality, I did not know if she would comprehend why my friend's personality did not allow her to expose her emotions in public—not even during a time of grief.

Differences in personalities might be the most important factor in determining how bereaved individuals express their grief. Some people will grieve silently; others will grieve openly and noisily. Neither mode of expression is a true indication of how much they are suffering internally.

* * *

Two points that cannot be stressed often enough are that each of us grieves in ways that are unique to us, and that no one has the right to judge the way in which another person is grieving.

If you are sincere in your desire to help bereaved individuals work through the grieving process, you will search for factors that make their grief their own. When you know these factors, you will better understand their grief, and the reasons why they are grieving in a specific way.

CHAPTER 3

The Emotions of Murdered-Child Grief

The pain is unexplainable, unbelievable, unacceptable.

Larry
9-5-95

We are in a rage and confused. We knew the suspect for about nine years. He has betrayed our trust in him.

Filiberto
1-23-96

CORE EMOTIONS THAT CAN TAKE ON ADDED DIMENSIONS

Although it can be said that death, like birth, is a normal and natural part of life, it is a subject that most of us tend to shy away from. Perhaps this is because of our innate will to survive, or our desire to live life to the fullest. Or perhaps it is because, even though most of us do hold some belief as to what occurs after death, it is still a factual unknown, and we are frightened by the unknown.

Despite our fear and our reluctance to discuss death, all of us will, at some point in our lives, suffer the death of a loved one. As we move through the grieving process, we will experience some, if not all, of the nine core emotions of grief.

The parents of a murdered child, teenager, or young adult also experience these emotions. However, due to the brutality and suddenness of their child's death, six of these emotions can take on added dimensions. They can become more complex and less easy to understand. Let me explain.

Shock

When their child is murdered, the parents are thrown into shock. After that numbing shock wears off, another kind of shock sets in.

We live in a society where the right to life, liberty, and the pursuit of happiness is protected under our Constitution. When these rights are taken away by an act of murder, the grieving parents form the belief that the murderer callously assumed that he or she had the right to kill, and also that that right superseded a child's rights to life and liberty, and a family's right to happiness. Forming this belief is normal under the circumstances, and it causes the parents to be shocked that someone assumed that he or she had the right to take their child's life.

Carolyn, whose twenty-four-year-old son was shot twice in the back and twice in the back of the head during the robbery of a bus station, explains, "My son's life was taken by another person," she says. "Someone who had no *RIGHT* whatsoever to do something so permanent and devastating. Something that destroyed his life and ours."

Elsie, the mother of a twenty-year-old woman who was brutally stabbed to death by an unknown assailant in her own home, agrees with Carolyn. "No one," adds Elsie, "has the *RIGHT* to decide when someone else should die."

Fear

Some parents fantasize avenging their child's death by killing the murderer. At first, they are stunned that they are capable of even thinking about committing this most horrendous of crimes. If the fantasies continue, and they sometimes do, the parents begin to feel fear. They can fear that they are not the decent persons they always believed themselves to be, or that their child's murder awakened a dark side of their personalities they never knew existed.

After my nineteen-year-old daughter was shot in the head by an unidentified male, I had such fantasies. I don't know which frightened me more—the malevolence of the fantasies themselves, or the reality that I was capable of having them. I pictured myself terrorizing the man who shot my daughter in the same way he had terrorized her. Then I would put a gun to his head and pull the trigger. In the beginning it terrified me that I could think such evil thoughts. Then I realized that my fantasy was a normal by-product of my grief. Having this fantasy allowed me to silently vent some of the rage and helplessness I was feeling.

Even though part of me fantasized shooting the man who shot my daughter, another part knew that, even if I had the opportunity, I would not be able to shoot him. An act of revenge such as this would not have brought my daughter back, but it would have made me just as base and depraved as the murderer. And if I was caught, convicted, and sentenced to prison, my absence would bring more crushing pain down upon the heads of my innocent family.

Anger

Anyone who experiences a loss feels anger. Bereaved persons can, for example, be angry with the paramedics or physicians who failed to save their loved one's life, or with other persons who have not suffered a loss and whose lives continue to be secure and happy, or with the person who died. Parents of a murdered child can feel this type of anger, and they might also feel angry with themselves.

Parents do not knowingly put their children into dangerous situations, or knowingly allow their children to place themselves in danger. When children do encounter danger and are murdered, their parents might blame themselves for not detecting the danger in advance. This blame can become self-anger.

Deena, whose two-year-old son was murdered by her ex-husband (the death certificate gives the cause of death as asphyxiation), has felt self-anger. She says, "I think another aspect of the grief feelings of a parent of a murdered child are the feelings of anger that one feels towards oneself. It took a long time to stop blaming myself or saying, 'What if. . . .' "

Self-anger is perhaps the most torturous emotion the parents can experience. They are not to blame for their child's death, and feeling that they are can increase their pain to a disabling level.

In addition to being in pain, the parents are weighted down by the agony of their grief and by the knowledge that their child was brutally murdered. Carrying this heavy burden leaves them with barely enough strength to function. Simple routines such as getting out of bed in the morning and taking a shower can leave them exhausted. Self-anger is an additional burden the parents must carry. It can sap what little strength they have—strength they will need to fight the long, arduous battle of surviving their grief.

Resentment

When children are born, their parents welcome them with a loving hello. When children die suddenly, the parents are cruelly denied the opportunity to say a loving goodbye. This denial is extremely traumatic, and that trauma can evolve into resentment.

Although it might be difficult for them to admit, the parents of a murdered child will sometimes resent other bereaved individuals who did have the opportunity to say goodbye to a deceased loved one. The parents who harbor this kind of resentment are emotionally torn in two. On one hand, they know that having the opportunity to say a loving goodbye *DEFINITELY* does not make the death any easier or less painful. Because of their own bereavement, they feel compassion for anyone whose loved one has died. On the other hand, the parents are resentful. They resent other people who had the opportunity to spend time with an ill or injured loved one—time during which they comforted their loved one—perhaps by fluffing their pillows, bringing them gifts, or by hugging and kissing them.

Parents of a murdered child feel cheated. There was no time to comfort their child. There were no pillows to fluff, no gifts to bring. The parents had no chance to ease their child's terror with hugs and kisses. The resentment they feel is neither spiteful nor self-serving. The parents should not be ashamed of being resentful, and other bereaved persons should not hold it against them. It is the result of the parents' grief and of their knowledge that their child felt terror and pain. It is a deep-seated yearning to go back to the time before their child was murdered and to prevent their child's lonely suffering.

Helplessness

The death of a child, teenager, or young adult is interpreted by many as being unnatural. Adults naturally expect to someday bury their parents, but they never expect to bury their child. When a child dies, the parents are left feeling completely helpless. They were unable to protect their child from death.

Because murder is also unnatural, it, when combined with the suddenness of their child's death, places an additional burden of pain on the parents. This, plus the fact that their child's life was taken away by a violent person, intensifies the helplessness they feel.

Carolyn's son was murdered in 1995. To date the murder remains unsolved. Her son is no longer alive. Her son's murderer is, and he walks about freely. He is enjoying the gift of life. These bitter realities increase Carolyn's feeling of helplessness. Although she constantly devises ways to keep the police focused on the investigation into her son's murder, she has been unsuccessful in bringing her son's killer to justice. Carolyn describes her feeling of helplessness. "I have had so many strong emotions since my son was murdered," she says. "They seem to come and go and change constantly, but I think by far one of the most powerful has to be helplessness. All my life as a mother, it seemed as though I could always fix everything that came along to trouble or hurt my child—to hold, comfort, and fix all problems. For the first time I cannot find a way to fix this."

Meaninglessness

Many of us ensure that our lives are well-rounded and worthwhile by engaging in meaningful careers and in numerous other activities. We value ourselves, and we consider our needs to be as important as the needs of our loved ones. But serving the needs of our loved ones, especially those of our children, is still an integral part of our lives. It, too, gives our lives meaning.

Parents spend the bulk of their time mentoring their children. Their mission in life is to advise and teach them. The act of mentoring fills the parents' lives with purpose.

According to some mental health professionals, the death of a child is the most traumatic loss a human being will ever suffer. This trauma is a double-edged blade. One edge of the blade severs the parents from the love and companionship of their child. The other edge severs them from the meaningful work of guiding their child into adulthood.

Most parents whose child has died agree with these mental health professionals. And so do I. I agree with them because I have experienced the deaths of several loved ones including my father, my mother, and my daughter. At the time of his death my father was seventy-five. My mother died at age eighty-two. After each of them died I was very sad, and I could not imagine life without them. When my daughter was murdered I wasn't just sad. I was desolate. There are valid reasons why the deaths of my parents did not affect me in the same way as my daughter's death. After I was married, even though my parents were still an important part of my world, they were no longer my primary family. My primary family was my husband and my children; they became the center of my world. More importantly, my body had not created my parents, but it had created my daughter. Not only had I created her, but her body had once been part of my body. When she was murdered my creation was destroyed. When she died part of me died too!

Jenny's seventeen-year-old daughter was shot in the back of the head by a young male armed with a stolen handgun. Since her daughter's death, Jenny has devoted her life to working with the families of homicide victims. She also agrees with these mental health professionals, but she takes their theory one step farther. "Based on my knowledge of victimization issues," she states, "I do know that the mere thought that someone else made a choice to end our loved one's life makes grief by homicide very different from any other type of death."

A homicide is a senseless and meaningless act. That the parents must live with the knowledge that someone senselessly ended their child's life adds another painful dimension to the emotion of meaninglessness.

EMOTIONS SPECIFIC TO MURDERED-CHILD GRIEF

In addition to experiencing the nine core emotions of grief, six of which, as I just explained, can take on added dimensions that increase their intensity, parents of murdered children also experience seven additional emotions that are specific to murdered-child grief. Although a combination of two or more of these emotions can be present in other types of grief, all of them are usually present in murdered-child grief. Some of these seven emotions can affect the parents more deeply than do the core emotions. They can be more painful, more debilitating, and more frightening.

Betrayal

Growing up we are taught that we live in a civilized society. Civilized means that we and our families are safe. Despite the violence we see at the movies or on the television, we believe that, in real life, civilized humans solve their differences with logic and verbal debate rather than with murder and mayhem. When faced with the harsh truth that all in society are not civilized, that one human being is capable of savagely taking the life of another, the parents feel betrayed.

Melanie, whose eighteen-year-old son was ambushed and gunned down by the former boyfriend of a girl her son was dating, says, "My son wanted to live, and someone chose to take his life in cold blood." Larry, Melanie's husband, adds, "My son begged him (the former boyfriend) not to take his life, but he murdered him anyway."

When a child is murdered intentionally, or as Melanie describes it, in cold blood, the parents view the safety of living in a civilized society as a cruel myth. The parents are civilized people, and they surrounded themselves and their child with civilized people. They did what was right and good and their goodness was betrayed. In one horrible moment, their child encountered a person who was not civilized, and in that moment their child was robbed of life.

Carol is another bereaved parent who feels betrayed. Approximately twenty-two years ago she, her husband, and two sons befriended a boy in need of foster care. At Carol's urging, her youngest son took this boy under his wing, and for fifteen years acted as his big brother. In 1989, when Carol's son was thirty-four, the boy he had lovingly guided into manhood broke into the son's home and shot him point-blank in the face with a twelve-gauge rifle. With his victim dead on the floor the murderer then stole cash, valuables, and the victim's car.

Carol is a caring and civilized person. When she saw a boy in need, she, with the help of her family, worked for two decades to satisfy that need. But her efforts to improve the life of one less fortunate than she were cruelly betrayed. Betrayed by a man who, instead of being grateful to Carol, repaid her kindness by murdering one of her beloved sons.

Deprivation

Parents treasure their children. They were created during an act of love. This creation took place within the mother's body. She nurtured, cared for, and protected her child prior to birth and afterwards. Deena believes that, "Our children are our most valuable and sacred belongings."

And how can parents not feel that their child belongs to them; the child is a unique individual that only that mother and father could have produced. There can never be another child like the child who was murdered.

The gift of life is our most precious commodity. Parents give their child life, and they struggle to make that life as fulfilling as possible. They hope that their struggle will be rewarded by having their child live a long, happy, and satisfying life. When their child is murdered, the parents are deprived of their reward, and their struggle is declared worthless by their child's murderer.

Deena explains that she felt deprivation when her young son was murdered. She was deprived of "a beautiful and loving child who brought nothing but joy to those he came in contact with."

Despair

At one time or another all humans have been afraid of the dark. Even as adults, many of us have perceived the black shadow cast by an inert object silhouetted in the moonlight as something menacing and frightening. Fortunately, this fear was quickly dispelled by turning on a light.

Murdered-child grief can be compared to a seemingly unending night of darkness and fear. There is no way this fear can be quickly dispelled. Before their child was murdered, the parents' lives were filled with happiness. After the murder, that happiness is replaced with sorrow. As the parents stumble through their sorrow, they begin to despair. They wonder if their lives will ever be happy again.

Carolyn describes despair as the most powerful of all her emotions since her son's death. "It has been," she says, "the most constant and consistent. There just isn't any hope left in me. No desire whatsoever to go on or to do anything. It seems as though I am wandering in a deep sea of blackness, and I can't find any light or any way out."

Distrust

More often than not, a murder is committed by a family member or by a person known to the victim. When this occurs the parents are horrified that their child was killed by someone who had a close association with them or their child.

Margie, whose twenty-seven-year-old daughter was stabbed twenty-four times by the daughter's husband, tells what it was like when she and her husband Kenneth were informed of their daughter's death. "When a priest and a member of the sheriff's department came to tell us that our daughter was murdered, and that they were holding her husband on suspicion of her murder, we became absolutely numb—and then gut-burning hysteria. We learned there was another side to our son-in-law, the man our daughter loved."

In cases such as this, the parents, while preparing for their child's funeral, can't help thinking back to their child's wedding. A wedding is an occasion of joy and celebration. During the ceremony the couple made a commitment to love, honor, and cherish. This type of commitment can be defined as a sacred trust. When that sacred trust is broken, in what can only be termed as the cruellest of ways, the emotional damage done to the parents is severe. Repairing this damage will be extremely difficult, and perhaps even impossible.

The strangulation death of the fourteen-year-old daughter of Helga and Filiberto is another instance where the alleged murderer was well known to both the victim and her family. "We watched him (the alleged murderer) grow into manhood," Filiberto explains sadly. "We used to socialize with his parents."

It is common for parents to entrust their children to family members, friends, and neighbors. The children are allowed to visit, to share a meal, and to play games. This socializing is natural and normal. It enriches the lives of the children. The thought that the people to whom the children are entrusted might be capable of murder never enters the minds of the parents or of the children. If parents cannot trust those who are close to them, whom can they trust? When that trust is broken by something as sadistic as a murder, the parents might never be able to trust again.

Deena, who has a daughter and two sons in addition to the son who was asphyxiated, states that she now has a very hard time trusting other people with her children. "I am over protective of my children," she says, "and insist on knowing where they are at all times." Deena's feeling of distrust makes life difficult for her living children as evidenced by her adolescent son who complains that she babies him.

Not being able to trust family members, friends, and neighbors is a horrible way to live. It is a devastating and extremely painful alteration to the parents' lives.

Disbelief

Many parents of murdered children believe that murder is an intentional act. Even when the murder is deemed to be accidental, they know that the killer initially made the *CONSCIOUS DECISION* to carry or to handle a weapon. Had the killer not made that conscious decision, they believe that their child would still be alive. Deena voices her feeling of disbelief. "My child died at the hands of another," she says, "and his death was intentional. It is hard to believe that anyone would want to take the life of someone so small and so innocent."

Margie also believes that her son-in-law intentionally took her daughter's life. "A person with a free will took a life," she states. "It was his choice."

Knowing that someone chose to take their child's life is the reason why so many parents, even though they do learn to live with their grief, never recover. Margie explains, "There is *NEVER* an end to this grief. There is no real recovery from this."

Anguish

All of us are familiar with anguish. Perhaps we have anguished over the possibility of losing our job, or if we should take on the long-term debt of buying a house, or if we will be able to send our children to college. Anguish can disturb our sleep. It can make us short tempered and irritable.

The parents of a murdered child also feel anguish. They anguish over the circumstances of their child's death. Margie describes her anguish. "Since my daughter was murdered, much of my time is spent wishing, *If I could have only been there to help her when she needed me.* A murder is so brutal. It is gut-wrenching to think of her being alone, to die alone and no one there to hold her hand, to hug her, to kiss her, to tell her how much she is loved."

This type of anguish is one of the reasons why murdered-child grief can last a lifetime. Margie's daughter was murdered in 1989, but she still uses the term, "to tell her how much she *IS* loved" as opposed to using the term, "to tell her how much she *WAS* loved." Margie will never stop loving her daughter, and she will never stop anguishing over the brutal way in which she died.

Rage

Rage is an emotion that is denounced by society and by most, if not all, religious communities. If the parents of a murdered child admit to being enraged by the savagery and senselessness of their child's death, they are often encouraged to forgive the murderer. Those who encourage the parents to forgive their child's murderer do not do so because they are rigidly sanctimonious. They do it because they are afraid for the grieving parents—afraid that their rage will permanently damage the parents physically and emotionally.

If the parents had a choice they would choose not to be enraged. It is an eroding and cumbersome emotion to live with. But these bereaved parents do not have a choice. Rage is a heavy chain they drag behind them—a chain made up of the horror of their child's murder and the myriad of painful grief emotions that burden them.

Many parents of a murdered child are enraged. Deena, who is but one of them, emphatically states that she was enraged with her ex-husband when he murdered her two-year-old son. "I wanted to rip his heart out with my bare hands," she says.

Chet, who at one time was the proud father of "a robust family of four sons," also feels rage. He became enraged after two of his four sons were brutally murdered in unrelated incidences. At age thirty-five, Chet's oldest son was attacked, stabbed, and shot by a disgruntled ex-employee who broke into the son's home demanding his job back. Eighteen months later, Chet's second son, also age thirty-five, was beaten and shot by a gang of youths who were not satisfied with the amount of money he was carrying when they robbed him. Chet explains that this gang of youths earned their living by robbing and murdering rather than by working. "They used the expression, 'It's payday.' or 'Let's go get paid.' " says Chet, "meaning they were entitled to whatever they could take from someone else."

Chet's sons were decent, productive members of society. When their lives were so savagely taken from them, Chet was filled with rage. Chet describes his rage as being, "A complete and utter rage that truly worthless individuals, who contribute nothing, can destroy good people." Chet is also enraged that the man who murdered his oldest son had "an extensive record of violent behavior" in two states, but was still allowed his freedom by the criminal justice system.

How can Deena and Chet, and other parents whose children were murdered, not be enraged? Their children were the innocent victims of violent and uncivilized predators. They will never stop loving their murdered children. They will never forget them. They will never forget the savagery of their child's death. How can they rid themselves of their rage when they cannot forget the brutal act that caused it?

* * *

Lois, whose twenty-four-year-old son was shot to death by an escaped convict hiding out in one of the townhouses being built by her husband and son, sums up, in one short sentence, what the murder of a child feels like to the child's parents. "It is," she says, "like an amputation without an anesthetic."

Her words bring to mind the gory scenes often shown in movies depicting the Civil War. Bloody scenes in which the arms and legs of wounded soldiers are sawed off, primitively and slowly, with only a shot of whiskey to ease their pain. In the movies these soldiers scream for relief. In real life, the parents of a murdered child scream for relief. In public, they scream silently. In private, they scream out loud.

CHAPTER 4

How the Parents of Murdered Children Deal with the Criminal Justice System

We accepted a plea bargain because there were no witnesses to my son's murder. There was enough evidence to go for second degree murder, but the District Attorney convinced us that, in our county, the shooter would be believed. If he didn't get convicted he would serve only one year or less.

Joan
3-13-96

We, the survivors of our children, continue to have to fight for our rights with the criminal justice system. We must work like hell to get petitions out and letters written to keep our children's murderers in prison for their full sentences.

Margie
12-4-95

We must also deal with the Parole System when the time comes for a parole hearing.

Rose
11-16-95

DEALING WITH THE POLICE

Recovering from grief can be one of life's most difficult battles. In order to win, the bereaved must confront and work through a maze of painful emotions. This is a convoluted process, one that takes an inordinate amount of time and energy.

The parents of a murdered child, like all other bereaved, want to conquer their grief and end their pain. In the beginning they cannot find the time and energy needed to do so; they are too busy interacting with the police and other branches of the criminal justice system. When Carol's son was murdered by the man her family had taken under its wing, she and her family barely had time to deal with the shock of his death and the burial. "We couldn't even begin to grieve," she explains, "until we waded through the justice system."

For some parents it can be years before they have the opportunity to begin working through their grief. Rose is one of those parents. Her twenty-two-year-old son was missing for sixteen months before his body was found buried in a shallow grave. With his wrists handcuffed behind his back, and his ankles bound together with a red, white, and blue necktie, he had been beaten to death by his college roommate, a man he considered to be his best friend. Like Carol, Rose put her grief aside so that she could deal with the criminal justice system. "I had to do this," she says, "because I wanted to make sure that justice was done for my child."

The first step in dealing with the criminal justice system is dealing with the law enforcement officers investigating the murder. If these officers are sensitive to the parents' shock and pain, they can provide them with important emotional support.

Deena has nothing but praise for the officers who investigated her young son's murder. "They did a good job of solving the case and were very quick about it," she says. "They were kind to me and tried to help me in whatever way they could."

Despite the horror of the situation, interacting with officers who are kind and helpful can be beneficial to the parents. Their lives have been shattered by a callous act of brutality, and they have lost faith in the goodness of mankind. The concern shown by officers, such as those who worked with Deena, helps to remind the parents that most humans are neither callous nor brutal.

There are instances, however, where the police are not as sensitive to the needs of the parents as they could be. The disappearance of Helga's and Filiberto's fourteen-year-old daughter caused them to be frightened and worried. "When her disappearance was reported to the police," says Filiberto, "they classified her as a run-away." This incorrect classification added insult to injury. Helga and Filiberto knew they had provided a warm and loving home for their daughter, and that she had no reason to run away.

When the police assume that a missing child or teenager has run away from home, the parents are caught in a catch-22 situation. On one hand, they know that the police usually classify a missing youth as a run-away because approximately two million youths do run away every year. On the other hand, the parents are frustrated because the police will not listen to them. The assumption that their child has run away is a generalization that infers there is something wrong in the home, and that the parents and the child are at odds.

After the body of Helga's and Filiberto's daughter was found the police did begin to investigate, but their frustration with the police did not end there. "At first," Filiberto explains, "we were not kept informed on the progress of the case." Eventually, with the help of a private investigator, this situation changed. "Now," continues Filiberto, "due to coordination between the private investigator and the local police, we have received updates on the progress of the case."

Law enforcement officers work hard, and they are sometimes buried under heavy case loads. Because of this, it is understandable that they might not be able to give the parents frequent updates. But the police must also understand the parents' feelings. They knew every detail of their child's birth and most of the details of their child's life. It naturally follows that they want to know the details of their child's death, as well as the details of the investigation.

Communication between the parents and the police can be a thorny issue. The investigating officers are busy gathering evidence, tracking leads, and interviewing witnesses and others who might have crucial information. The parents are in shock and are desperate to know who murdered their child. Communication between these two parties is going to be difficult, but it is necessary. Perhaps the needs of both can be met if ground rules are established when the investigation begins. The officers can inform the parents of their willingness to speak with them and suggest the best time of day or evening to call. They can ask the parents to refrain from calling at other times. Usually, when the parents know that they will be receiving regular updates, they will cooperate. These phone contacts need not be long and drawn out. The parents can quickly be apprised of the latest developments in the case and assured that the investigation is moving forward.

Some parents, because of their need to know every detail of their child's murder, choose not to rely on the police as their sole source of information. Mary is one of these parents. In 1988 her eighteen-year-old son was sexually assaulted and beaten to death while visiting prospective colleges in California. After the murder, Mary and her husband, on four separate occasions, traveled from their East coast home to the site of the crime. "While there," she says, "we were very vocal. We asked questions of the homeless people living on the campus of the high school where our son was murdered. We also spoke to the students there, met with the coroner, visited the District Attorney's office, and researched the killer's criminal history." During one of these visits, Mary learned that, shortly after her son was murdered, his killer was caught by the unified school district police in the act of sodomizing a fourteen-year-old boy on the same spot where he had beaten her son to death. "The police obviously allowed the murderer to live on the campus," she continues, "and knew him."

All parents react differently to the murder of their child. When those like Mary choose to visit the scene, and to speak with anyone who might have information, the police can help them survive their grief by cooperating fully.

Law enforcement officers do solve many murdered-child cases, and they are to be commended for their expertise and diligence. However, there are some cases the police are not able to solve quickly.

When a murder remains unsolved, the parents describe their experience with the police as being unsatisfactory. They wonder why the investigation is not producing the desired result. Doubts, that on the surface might seem unreasonable to other people, run through the parents' minds: *Are the police doing everything they possibly can? Is my family not high-profile enough to warrant an aggressive investigation? Is the media not putting pressure on the police to solve my child's murder?* The parents have suffered a tragedy they never thought they would. Prior to the murder they had no reason to distrust, but now they do. Under these circumstances the parents' doubts are not unreasonable. If they verbalize them to the police or to family members and friends, they should not be criticized or chastised. Many parents, because the death of their child has rendered their lives meaningless, will attempt to find new meaning by ensuring that the police keep the investigation open for as long as it takes to bring their child's killer to justice.

Carolyn, who has been waiting since 1995 for the police to determine who shot her son, hopes that the case will be solved in the near future. "This is the one thing that keeps me going," she says. "If only I can think up some way or some thing to keep the case alive and moving."

When an investigation is several months old, the police might not have any new information to give to the parents. If this is the case, the parents begin to fear that the police are no longer working to solve their child's murder. This fear becomes an added burden the parents must carry. Their pain worsens and their despair deepens.

Although Carolyn continues to be hopeful she has also begun to fear. "My husband and I just can't seem to get any information from the detectives," she explains. "They seem to push us aside as excess baggage or something. If only they could understand how much this means to us."

Unsolved cases traumatize the parents of a murdered child in other ways as well. They question why, in this technologically-advanced age of forensic science, the police have been unable to gather sufficient evidence to solve the crime.

Elsie's daughter was stabbed to death in 1982, but the murder remains unsolved. Intellectually, Elsie knows that her daughter is dead, but emotionally she cannot fully accept that her daughter was murdered. "Sometimes," she says, "it still doesn't seem real."

An unsolved case is like an unfinished book. There is no final chapter—no arrest, no trial, no punishment—that allows Elsie, and parents in the same situation, to close the book on their child's murder. Instead of finding closure, they continue to be consumed by a burning desire to know who savaged their child and by the knowledge that the killer moves about freely enjoying life. As long as the parents are distracted in this way they cannot focus on working through their grief. And when there is no alleged killer for the parents to confront in a court of law, it is hard for them to confront the reality that another human was actually capable of murdering their child.

In spite of the parents' inability to focus on working through their grief, they do manage to survive the trauma of their child's murder. And they do manage to go on with their lives. Surviving is definitely much less desirable than recovering, but it is the best these parents can do. The secret of their survival is their ability to focus in on their yearning to close the book on their child's murder. Carolyn focuses on her hope that her son's killer will someday be caught and punished. Elsie focuses on a statement made to her by one of the investigating officers. "He used a saying, 'What comes round, goes round,' when speaking about the case," she explains. "My faith has sustained me throughout this horror, and someday the person or persons who are responsible for taking my daughter's life *WILL* pay!"

Christina and Evelyn are bereaved mothers who also describe their experiences with the police as being unsatisfactory. Their daughters were murdered many years ago. Both cases are unsolved.

On a March night in 1976, at approximately 9:00 P.M., Christina's seventeen-year-old daughter accepted a ride home from a bus stop with someone the police believe the daughter knew. The ride ended with her being raped, beaten, and run over by a car. Christina believes the police were unable to solve this crime because they honed in on male members of her family rather than searching for other males her daughter might have known. Although Christina's daughter was murdered many years ago, she still mourns her daughter's death. "I often break down because my grief is still so bad," she says. "I wonder why and what happened. Will I ever know? I like to be alone sometimes to think. And to cry just like I am doing now."

Evelyn's nineteen-year-old daughter was missing for a week. When her body was found the cause of death was listed as undetermined. One year later, in 1985, the body was exhumed, and it was determined that Evelyn's daughter had been stabbed. Evelyn is in conflict. Not knowing the cause of her daughter's death was torture. Although she credits the perseverance of one of the investigating officers with ending her torture, she is still dissatisfied with the system that has not yet been able to bring her daughter's killer to justice.

Carolyn, Elsie, Christina, and Evelyn wait for their children's murders to be solved. We all know what it is like to wait. Even though we might be waiting for something good to happen, the wait can be nerve-wracking. Parents who wait month after month, year after year, for their child's murder to be solved, are in agony. They desperately yearn to begin working through their grief, but their rage with the unknown killer and their dissatisfaction with the police makes it impossible for them to do so.

These parents eventually learn to live with the trauma of their child's murder; they assimilate it into their lives. By assimilating, they might appear to be leading normal, happy lives, and people who come in contact with them are fooled into believing that the parents have recovered. This increases the parents' feelings of isolation and loneliness. They are trapped inside an invisible bubble of grief and have little hope of finding a way to free themselves.

DEALING WITH THE COURT SYSTEM

When the murder has been solved and an arrest has been made, the parents begin preparing to attend the alleged murderer's trial.

At this point, family members and friends can easily mistake the parents' satisfaction with knowing that the alleged murderer is behind bars, for what they believe is the parents' readiness to begin battling their grief. But the parents know they are far from ready. Preparing to attend the trial is a battle in itself, one that presents a new set of hurtful problems.

Much to the parents' dismay, they soon learn that they might have to wait months, or even years, for the trial to begin. Helga's and Filiberto's daughter was strangled to death in 1994, but, two years later, they still did not know when her alleged murderer would stand trial. The reason they did not know was this: A date, upon which the actual date that the trial is to begin, is set. This date is called the trial scheduling date. Often, this trial scheduling date, which again, does nothing more than set the date of the trial, is postponed. Sometimes, as in the case of Helga and Filiberto, this scheduling date is postponed time and time again. Every time this scheduling date is moved farther into the future, the trial date is moved farther into the future.

When the parents must wait for such a long time, due to numerous delays and postponements, they must continue to put their grief on hold. They do not have the strength to confront their grief while enduring the anguish of waiting.

For the majority of parents, the murder of their child is their first exposure to the criminal court division of the justice system. When this division moves along at a snail's pace, when it allows—and even seems to condone—numerous delays and postponements, the parents become disillusioned. They want the attorneys and judges who make up the criminal court division to acknowledge their excruciating pain and to understand that the trial is going to cause them additional trauma. They want the trial to be over and done with, but they are powerless to make this happen. The powerlessness they are feeling rekindles the powerlessness they felt when their child was murdered. Their pain increases, and their despair deepens.

While waiting to stand trial, the alleged killer usually spends time in prison. Some criminal justice systems consider this time to be *time served. Time served* is then deducted from the sentence handed down if the alleged murderer is found guilty. Jenny explains that the state in which she resides has what is known as *good time*. "Good Time," she says, "knocks 30 percent off of a prisoner's time going in after he or she is convicted."

But no criminal justice system acknowledges the fact that, prior to the trial, the parents of the murdered child are also spending time in prison. Their prison is not surrounded by high stone walls topped with barbed wire and it does not contain cells made of iron bars, but it might as well. The parents' days and evenings are spent in an unseen cell. They must stay close to the phone and the mail box or risk missing notification of a postponement, or rescheduling, or even the date of the trial. If a caring family member, friend, therapist, or physician suggests that the parents go away for a few days of much needed rest, the parents must ignore this wise suggestion. They are not free to come and go as they please; their movements are dictated by the attorneys and judges who control the criminal justice system. The parents' lives, as well as their grief, are put on hold. Unlike the convicted criminal, this time is never given back to the parents. They lose it just like they lost their child.

On the surface, the term *good time,* when used to denote prison time that is deducted from a convicted killer's sentence, seems innocuous. But when it is examined in depth, it becomes apparent that this term is hurtful to the parents of the murdered child. Before their child died, the parents' lives were filled with good times and happiness; the years ahead of them were aglow with hopes and dreams. After the murder, there is nothing *good* about the parents' lives. The bright flames of their happiness, of their hopes and dreams, have been extinguished by the convicted killer. And yet some legislators, attorneys, and judges, despite knowing that the parents will never again have a completely good time, coin and use this hurtful term. The parents become more disillusioned with a system that, on many levels, seems to be insensitive to their pain and suffering.

While waiting for the trial to begin, the parents anguish over what is going to occur in court. Mentally, they attempt to prepare themselves for the horror of seeing vividly colored, poster size photographs of the crime scene, of their child's mutilated body, and of the autopsy. But deep in their hearts they know that the photographs they briefly conjure up in their minds are nothing more than edited versions of the real thing. Their pain will not allow them to fully visualize the injuries their child sustained, and their minds will not allow them to dwell on visions of their child's lifeless body.

The parents also attempt to prepare themselves for the horror of sitting in the same room with the alleged killer. They know that every breath this person takes is going to remind them that their child breathes no more.

And they dread having to hear the police and other expert witnesses describe the murder and the damage done to their child's body. To the parents, their child's death is a highly emotional issue. To the expert witnesses, it is little more than another part of their normal workday. The parents wish they were the expert witnesses rather than the mother and father of the murdered child. After these witnesses give their testimony, they will exit the courtroom and reenter a world filled with love and laughter. When the parents exit the courtroom, their lives will still be filled with emptiness and sorrow. Their child will still be dead. For the remainder of their lives memories of the trial will be their constant companions. They will never be able to erase from their minds the horrors of what they saw and heard in the courtroom.

Sitting through the alleged killer's trial evokes feelings within the parents they will seldom admit in public. They would not wish their agony on anyone, and they would do anything they could to prevent another parent's child from being murdered. But, at the same time, they come into the courtroom with the knowledge that some parents ignore or abuse their children, and even abandon them. The parents of the murdered child can't help feeling that this tragedy should have happened to one of those parents.

To those who have never suffered the murder of a loved one, these feelings might seem shamefully selfish. But they are not. The parents are still reeling from the shock of their child's death. They are still struggling to accept the fact that their child was murdered; a hard task when they long so desperately for their child to still be alive.

Some people who are worried about the mental and physical health of the parents might question why they force themselves to sit through the trial if it increases their pain. These people ask this question because they are afraid this added torture will cause the parents permanent emotional damage. The parents attend the trial for the same reason other parents endure the pain of holding their child on their laps while the child is being given an inoculation or having a laceration sutured. These parents want to see that their child is given proper medical treatment in the exact same way the parents of a murdered child want to see that justice is done for their child.

DEALING WITH FLAWS AND WEAKNESSES IN THE CRIMINAL JUSTICE SYSTEM

Parents who do not have to wait extended periods of time for their child's murder to be solved and the trial to be over consider themselves to be lucky. They hope that the conviction and sentencing will bring closure, and they are eager to begin working through the grief process. But when their luck turns from good to bad, as it frequently does, they realize that a more severe heartache lies ahead.

Following are some of these bad luck stories. As you read them, please remember that they are not embellished in any way, and that the parents telling the stories are people just like you, who, before their children were murdered, were living what can be described as normal lives.

If you have a close association with the parents of a murdered child, the anguish they are feeling is already causing you anguish. You would like nothing more than to ease their pain, but you are powerless to do so. Because of this close association, you are going to connect to these bad luck stories. They are going to cause you more anguish. When you are finished reading, you might ask why you were not aware that many laws provide gaping loopholes that allow convicted murderers to avoid punishment equal to the brutality of their crimes. The subject of murder is a frightening one. No one likes to think about it. If we did, we would live in constant fear, and the quality of our lives would be diminished greatly. No one wants to live in fear. No one wants to think that one of their loved ones might someday be murdered. And so, understandably, we remain ignorant of the flaws in our criminal justice systems.

Beckie, whose eighteen-year-old son was robbed of his wallet and then shot to death while walking his girlfriend home from work, became aware of some of these flaws in the most devastating of ways. "We thought we were *lucky* that the three people involved with our son's death had been caught and jailed by the fifth day after the murder," she says, "but that was where our *luck* ended. Mistakes made by the detectives and the prosecutor eventually ended with the eighteen-year-old man who actually shot our son serving only seven years."

Three young men participated in the robbery. "My son," Beckie continues, "asked them if he could keep his drivers license, and the eighteen-year-old gunman answered with a bullet from a .357 Magnum to my son's shoulder. My son then handed over his wallet, and the eighteen-year-old shot him again in the center of his chest. My son died instantly. The man who murdered him is serving only seven years. But another one of the men, a seventeen-year-old, is serving twenty years for his part in the robbery."

Such disparities in sentencing make no sense to the parents of a murdered child. If you are not a legislator, a criminal attorney, or a judge they probably make no sense to you either. It is hard to understand why a man who chose to carry a gun and to deliberately pull the trigger—not once, but twice—is sentenced to serve so much *less* time than a man who only participated in the same crime. It is hard to understand why the legislators who write and enact our laws allow mistakes made by detectives and prosecutors to go in favor of a cold-blooded killer and against the innocent victim. It is hard to understand why the criminal justice system mocks the agonizing reality that a child has been murdered by allowing the killer to walk out of prison seven years after he committed the murder—a senseless act of violence.

Beckie feels that she, her family, and her murdered son have been victimized four times. Once by the killer, once by the detectives, once by the prosecutors, and once by the court. "This revictimization by the entire judicial system compounds my family's grief" she says.

Beckie's story of injustice is one of sheer horror. The one told by Patricia is just as horrible. Her daughter was murdered in 1992. "A man my daughter knew was caught attempting to molest her daughter," states Patricia. "My daughter was prosecuting him, and he stated if he had to do time in jail he would kill her. He stalked her for approximately six weeks and was jailed several times. But he always got bailed out and harassed her. Ultimately he entered my daughter's house and killed her by stabbing her primarily in the throat."

The man who murdered Patricia's daughter was arrested and stood trial for the killing. However, the attempted molestation, the repeated stalkings, and his previous arrests were not allowed into evidence. She explains this was because the police had dropped the original case—Gross Sexual Imposition—against this man. "And," she continues, "the prosecutor could not ask for the death penalty because the murderer chased my daughter out of her dwelling and inflicted the fatal wound on the porch. In this state there must be two felonies committed *in the same dwelling,* and my daughter was on the porch."

Here again the parents of murdered children cannot understand why such important events, events that explain why the murder was committed, are not allowed to be heard during the trial. To them, preventing the judge or jury from considering such crucial information is like draining the gasoline from the tank of a car and then expecting the engine to operate properly without it. Neither can they understand why the brutal stabbing death of a young mother is not worthy of the death penalty just because the stabbing began inside the house and ended on the porch that is attached to the house. To them murder is murder regardless of where and when the victim died. The place of death is irrelevant to the pain the grieving parents are feeling—until they are told that their child's killer will, at some point in the near future, be allowed to walk out of prison and to resume his or her life. Then it becomes agonizingly relevant.

The list of horror stories goes on and on:

Deena—The man who asphyxiated her two-year-old son was sentenced to seventeen years to life. "When he is eligible for parole," says Deena, "my son, had he lived, would only be about twenty years old. This is still very young."

Melanie—The seventeen-year-old who ambushed and executed her son for dating his former girlfriend was found guilty of first degree, premeditated murder and is now serving a life sentence. "Not life without parole as he deserves," Melanie states angrily. "He could be released in approximately thirteen years. The judicial system really stinks. Some of these judges are pitiful."

Carol—The less fortunate man whose life she and her family attempted to improve for fifteen years, plea bargained and received five to fifteen years in a medium security facility. "Then," states Carol, "he went to a work camp, and from there a halfway house after which he was paroled. My son is dead *forever!* His murderer is out on parole. Is this justice? I call it injustice!"

Chet—The disgruntled ex-employee who had a long history of violent behavior prior to killing Chet's first son was found guilty of first degree murder. "He was given a life sentence which means he was eligible for parole in twenty years," states Chet. "But then, three and one-half years later, some people who wanted to use him as a hit man helped him to escape from prison. When he was recaptured he was sentenced to twenty years consecutive with his previous sentence. So now it will be forty-three years before he can apply for parole."

—Two of the gang members who murdered Chet's second son, because they pervertedly believed they were entitled to the money he had earned legitimately, were found guilty of first degree murder. "Both," says Chet, "were given life sentences instead of death. They could both be back on the streets before they're forty years old. I am enraged at a system that allows monsters to walk the streets."

Jenny—"The man who murdered my daughter pled guilty to first degree manslaughter. There was no trial. First degree manslaughter carries a maximum sentence of forty-one *months*. The sentencing judge gave this man the full forty-one months but he served only twenty-seven months. In my eyes, that is not much for taking a life. I would have liked him to be charged with second degree murder. However, the prosecutor felt the evidence did not support that this man *intended* to murder my daughter. My thought is: 'What does one exactly intend to do when they hold a loaded, cocked gun to someone's head?' My family, my daughter, and her friends all got a life sentence. Why didn't he?"

Beckie, Patricia, Deena, Melanie, Carol, Chet, and Jenny are enraged that their children's murderers were all given sentences that either allowed or will allow them to resume their lives outside of prison. To understand why these parents feel rage, picture your own children or grandchildren, your nieces or nephews. In your mind look into their innocent faces. Listen to the sound of their laughter. See them at work or at play. Feel their arms hugging you tightly. Then consider the violent ways in which the children of these parents died, and imagine the children you are picturing in your mind dying in similar ways. When the face of a young murder victim is replaced with the face of a child, teenager, or young adult whom you love, you too will feel deep sorrow and anger. Then, when you realize that the person who murdered the child you love will probably walk free after being incarcerated for only a short time, and will, perhaps, murder another child, you too will feel rage.

All too often the parents of a murdered child, teenager, or young adult are told that the motive for their child's murder was rage. The person who killed was born into an economically deprived family, or lost a job or a relationship, or held political beliefs not endorsed by the majority. And so they vented their rage on innocent people. Their rage is their excuse for committing murder. Why then don't the parents of a murdered child vent their rage in the same obscene way? Why don't they murder their child's murderer? The answer is simple. The parents do not believe that they have the right to kill. That they are good people who do not avenge their child's death with a retaliatory act of violence can be a bitter pill for them to swallow. On one level, they would like to punish their child's killer because they have lost faith in the ability of our criminal courts to mete out punishment equal to the crime. On another level, they realize that if they take the law into their own hands they would be helping to create a society of anarchists. These conflicting feelings torture the parents. Their pain increases, and their despair deepens.

* * *

"If the parents of a murdered child are not the aggressors they get nothing." These words are spoken by Mata.

Mata's twenty-one-year-old daughter was kidnapped from her place of employment by a man who wanted to date her. This man drove Mata's daughter ten miles to a reservoir. There he crushed her skull with a tire iron. Then he strangled her, and finally he drowned her. "This man was very violent toward women," explains Mata. "I think he approached my daughter, and when she said no, he decided to show her who was the boss. I feel he meant to kill her."

When her daughter died, Mata became a changed person. She is now acutely aware that anyone can be murdered. She has experienced the destruction and devastation of a brutal killing firsthand. Mata's voice could be the voice of any parent whose child has been murdered. "We must educate people on what we all go through when our child is murdered," she says. "We also must work toward better laws and *Justice for all of us.*"

CHAPTER 5

Ways in Which the Lives of Parents of Murdered Children Permanently Change

Death is forever, and the pain goes on forever!

Carol
11-20-95

We will continue to "recover" for the rest of our lives.

Mary
3-9-96

When we discuss the murder of a child, we describe the child as *the victim*. However, if we are to understand murdered-child grief, we need to begin thinking of the parents as *victims* also. In a literal sense, the parents are not dead. But they, too, have been injured; the murder has created permanent changes in their lives.

Although some parents interpret a few of these changes as positive—perhaps because they must find small shreds of hope in order to survive the trauma of their child's murder—for the most part, they interpret the changes as negative.

NEGATIVE CHANGES

Permanent Voids

From the moment of death, a child's murder creates voids in the parents' lives—voids that can never be filled.

It snatches away a part of their present. "I miss seeing my daughter on a daily basis," explains Jenny, "touching her, smelling her hair, hugging her, talking with her for hours on end. I miss going to the movies with her. I miss eating popcorn with her. I miss tickling her and having her tickle me. I miss her jumping out from behind doors and scaring me and then having her laugh so hard about it. I miss telling her I love her. I miss her telling me that she loves me."

What Jenny has described are small gestures of love she and her daughter shared. Other parents shared similar gestures with their child—gestures that added warmth, substance, and pleasant noise to their everyday lives. Without them, the parents' days are filled with blank, silent spaces. No other arms can provide the same kind of warmth. No other activity can fill the blanks. No other voice can dispel the silence.

Their child's death also snatches away a chunk of the parents' future. They will never have the opportunity to revel joyously during certain events—the birthdays and graduations that will never be celebrated, the wedding that will never be planned, the good news of a job promotion, and other accomplishments that will never be shared. And it snatches away chunks of future generations. Pam's only daughter was shot to death at age twenty-two during a robbery that took place in the daughter's home. "She never married," says Pam, "and she had no children. I will miss the grandchildren she would have given me." For the remainder of their lives, the parents will paint pictures of birthday parties, graduations, and the births of a grandchild and a great-grandchild in their minds. They will long for these pictures to become real. They will feel the pain of being denied these events and the pleasure they would have brought.

The passage of time does not erase their child from the parents' thoughts. Deena's two-year-old son was asphyxiated in 1987. "I think about him a lot," she says. "What would he have been like now?" As the parents envision their child at different ages and in a variety of situations, they feel cheated and betrayed. It's as if someone handed them an armful of gift-wrapped packages filled with wondrous surprises the day their child was born, and shortly afterward, told them that the packages can never be opened.

Painful Reminders

The loss of sharing small gestures of love and future events with their child are but two of the permanent negative changes the parents must endure. They might someday accept the reality of their child's murder and begin to assimilate it into their lives, but, like the amputee who continues to feel the presence of an amputated limb and to miss it, the parents will continue to miss their child. They, and their lives, will always be diminished. Even though Christina's daughter was raped and beaten to death over twenty years ago, Christina still suffers.

"Many, many nights I sob into my pillow," she says. "I feel hopeless and helpless. I wonder what each day will be like."

Because each day of the parents' new lives begins as a mystery—will a sight, a smell, or a sound they encounter that day trigger a bout of pain so severe it temporarily renders them immobile—some parents, at least for a while, have trouble making plans for the future. They know that in order to survive they must concentrate their energies on coping with the here and now. Filiberto states that, since their daughter was strangled to death in July of 1994, he and his wife Helga now live one day at a time. "We have no goal in life since we lost our daughter," he explains.

Sights and sounds that were once nothing more than a backdrop to life, have moved to center stage and they have the power to remind the parents of the homicide. "Seeing the school bus bothers us," continues Filiberto, "and the high school our daughter would have attended. Also the shopping malls. And seeing young teenagers."

Certain smells can affect parents in the same way. When my daughter was seven years old, she began to study voice and guitar. By the time she was seventeen, she had gained sufficient expertise to become a member of a professional top-forty rock band that traveled up and down the East coast to perform. Her favorite flower was the yellow rose, and very often, the bookcase in her bedroom held a vase of yellow roses sent by an admirer. The scent of a rose still makes me feel sad despite the fact that she was shot in the head over thirteen years ago. It reminds me of how much I miss her. And, as much as I hate it, I find myself replaying the brutality of her murder in my mind.

Places the parents visited with their child can also become painful reminders. "I no longer enjoy doing certain things," explains Pam, "like going to the beach or listening to the radio. These are things my daughter and I did together."

The parents know that certain sights, sounds, smells, and places will always remind them of their murdered child. But, because they yearn to remember their child with joy rather than despair, they hope the passage of time will eventually enable them to do so. Until it does, they continue to be immersed in the battle to conquer their grief. They must, like Helga and Filiberto, settle for living their lives one day at a time.

Dread of the Future

Although the parents are unable to make plans for the future, they do think about the future—with dread. They dread the arrival of Mother's Day, Father's Day, and most holidays. "There are no

Christmas cheers in our house," explains Filiberto. "We cannot wait until the holidays pass." While other parents are complaining that the holidays do not last long enough the parents of a murdered child feel that they drag on forever. They can't wait for them to be over. "Holidays will never be the same," says Jenny.

The parents also dread the arrival of other significant days. "We have to face our daughter's birthday and the date of her death," comments Filiberto. For years to come the parents will, on these significant dates, relive the events that occurred. In their mind's eye, they will watch the clock and they will remember, in great detail, what happened at what time. They will no longer feel joy on their child's birthday, and the date of their child's death is even worse. The agony they feel will eventually subside to a dull ache, but they will never stop hurting completely. The parents would definitely prefer not to dredge up the painful past, but they cannot help themselves. They cannot stop the memories from rising up in their minds any more than they can stop the sun from rising up in the morning sky.

Physical Health Problems

Beyond every bend in the unfamiliar road the parents are traveling, there seems to lurk another negative change. During the turmoil of the investigation, the trial, and the sentencing they might begin to experience physical changes. Carol's son was murdered by the less-fortunate man her family tried to help in November of 1989. In 1990 she and members of her family were forced to undergo treatment for a variety of illnesses. "All of us," says Carol, "were under constant medical care for ulcers, stress-related skin conditions, fatigue, insomnia, and arthritic flare-ups." Carol believes that these physical problems were caused by emotional distress. She continues, "At the same time, all of us were experiencing bouts of anger, guilt, sadness, loneliness, depression, frustration, and intense rage." In 1992 Carol developed cancer. She also believes that the ordeal of her son's murder and all that occurred afterward continued to weaken her body to the point where she was susceptible to this fatal illness. Between the time of her son's death and the diagnosis of her cancer, Carol, along with her husband, founded and facilitated a chapter of a nationwide support group for the parents of murdered children. "We thought we were dealing well with the murder by helping others," she says, "but the murderer will end up killing me too!"

Mary also developed a rare form of cancer two years after her son was sexually assaulted and beaten to death. Like Carol, she believes that her cancer is the direct result of the many ways in which she suffered emotionally during those two years. "The death of my son caused much dissension and hurt in the family, and broken hearts," she explains, "and perhaps the premature deaths of his maternal grandparents."

Some physicians speculate that our emotions and outlook on life can have a powerful effect on our physical health. So it seems logical that the parents' physical health might be damaged by their negative emotions. For years to come, because they are the victims of a homicide, they will live in turmoil. Their lives will be a living hell.

Loss of Interest in Life

Before their child was murdered, the parents' lives were normal and happy. Each day—although there were high points and low points—was similar to the day before. The sameness of each day gave them a sense of security and comfort. After the murder, they no longer feel either secure or comfortable. Instead they feel anguish and pain. These negative emotions are the exact opposite of the positive emotions they felt before the murder. They can change the parents' outlook on everyday life. "Prior to my daughter's murder, my circle of friends considered me the clown, the social director, always planning a party or get together, not one to take life seriously," explains Jenny. "I am no longer that person. I am much quieter and have a much more serious outlook on life."

Carolyn's outlook on life has also changed. "My feelings and reactions are completely different now than they were before my son was murdered," she says. "The things that meant so much to me before mean nothing to me now. I am not the same person, but a stranger."

Losing interest in activities, events, and enterprises that once gave purpose to their lives can frighten the parents. When they realize that the pleasures they once considered to be so important now have no meaning, they might become despondent. They fight their despondency by forcing themselves to talk, to smile, to walk, and to function. By pretending to lead lives that appear to be normal, and by keeping busy, the parents attempt to fit into the world of the non-bereaved. But when they are alone with their grief, or are sharing their grief with members of their support groups, they know that in many ways they do not fit in. They can hide their ongoing feelings of grief from the outside world by building a facade of happiness. But behind that facade, they know that all future happiness will be marred by the absence of their child. Chet comments that since two of his four sons were murdered, he is only going through the motions of living. "I don't enjoy anything. Activities, people, food," he says. "I pretend, but I really don't care."

When the parents state that they *are only pretending to enjoy life,* they can be revealing two more of the permanent changes that have taken place in their lives.

First, the negative emotions of anguish and agony are so strong they crowd out all positive emotions. Although the positive emotions will gradually return, they will always be overshadowed by the permanent emotional damage the homicide has done to the parents. They will never again be able to fully enjoy the benefits of their positive emotions.

Second, the parents might feel guilty. They are alive. Their child is dead. This is definitely not the way it was supposed to be. Chet continues, "If I feel as if I might be having a good time I feel guilty." Those people who have not experienced murdered-child grief can have a hard time understanding this guilt. The parents did not commit the murder. They would have gladly given their own lives to preserve their child's. Regardless of these realities, the parents know that their child will never again have a good time. Their guilt is a manifestation of their desire to have their child back with them and of their frustration at not having been able to prevent their child's death.

Loss of Trust

The murder of a child, teenager, or young adult is a heinous crime. Its savagery is indelibly burned into the parents' minds. Patricia will never forget the horror she felt in June of 1992 when her daughter was stabbed to death. "I think about it every day," she says.

The emotional wounds the parents have sustained will never completely heal. Their pain will eventually ease but, to some degree, they will always suffer. Their view of the world and the people in it will permanently change.

The majority of us believe that mankind is inherently good. We see goodness all around us. Some people devote their lives to helping those less fortunate or those who are mentally or physically ill. Others obey the law, work hard to earn a living, take good care of their families, and never intentionally hurt another person. We believe in the inherent goodness of mankind because we are good. We know that we are incapable of harming another person and we trust that others will not harm us. We lead decent lives and, in return, we expect to be treated decently.

Most parents, because they believe in the goodness of mankind, strive to develop the qualities of kindness and caring they see in their children to the highest possible level. Beckie is one of these parents. She encouraged her son to be kind and caring. When he was callously gunned down he was performing an act of kindness. He was escorting his girlfriend home from work. When her son died, Beckie suffered two losses. "I lost my son," she explains, "and I lost my trust in the world."

Jenny's view of the world has also changed. "I know now that I can't be sure of anything," she states. "I am not as trusting as I was before."

When the parents lose their faith in the goodness of mankind and their trust in the world, they feel betrayed. Some parents also feel that they have been betrayed by the criminal justice system. The twenty-two-year-old man who murdered Mary's son in 1988 was on probation in California. "He was on probation for robbery and sexual imposition," she says. "The sexual imposition charge was plea bargained to simple robbery." While on probation the murderer took it upon himself to travel to Ohio. There he was again arrested for gross sexual imposition and robbery. He was sentenced to three to fifteen years in prison, but an Ohio judge reduced this sentence to probation because, he claimed, he had no knowledge of a previous criminal history. The murderer then asked the judge if he could return to California to serve his Ohio probation and the judge allowed him to do so. "It is my understanding that this type of action is referred to as regional dumping," continues Mary. "Naturally, left to his own devices, the criminal disappeared. The next time this depraved human being surfaced our son was dead." Despite the multiple violent crimes of which this young offender has been convicted, the criminal justice system has proposed releasing him from prison before his full sentence has been served. This proposal, which Mary is fighting, reinforces her loss of trust in her fellow man.

Alterations in Lifestyle

When a child has been murdered, the parents' old lives come to an abrupt end and they must begin the long hard journey toward new ones. Working through their grief is the first leg of that journey. It is the period of transition that ferries them from the past to the future.

As the parents begin to journey toward their new lives they strive to retain bits and pieces of their old lives. They do not want to lose meaningful relationships they share with family members and friends, or to be denied the pleasure of hobbies and pastimes they have always enjoyed. In some ways the parents are still the same people they were before the homicide. But in other ways they are quite different, and they might need to live their new lives differently. Jenny explains, "My husband and I used to go out on the town a lot, but now we rarely do so. We prefer quiet evenings at home, or small gatherings with friends."

Alterations in the parents' lifestyles can be necessary to the successful completion of the grieving process. But such alterations can increase their feelings of sadness and loss. These alterations can also unsettle the people who once participated in certain activities with them. Understandably, because family members, friends, co-workers, and others have not suffered the murder of their child, they cannot fully comprehend the magnitude of the upheaval that has taken place in the parents' lives. They cannot fully comprehend the ways in which the parents have changed. Becoming familiar with, and accustomed to these changes takes time and patience. The parents' progression through the grieving process becomes a period of transition not only for them, but for all who know them.

Ongoing Anger

When the parents of a murdered child feel that they have been betrayed by the murderer and by the criminal justice system, and that they can no longer trust the world or the people in it, they become angry. Although they might attempt to hide their anger from the outside world, it is revealed in their responses to certain situations. Since Deena's son was murdered in 1987, she has been studying the criminal justice system. "I don't believe in criminals' civil rights," she says, "and can become quite *mean* on the subject."

Mary, remembering that her son was savagely beaten and sexually assaulted prior to his death, felt anger when she learned that some people in the state where she resides expressed concern that incarcerated criminals might be experiencing sensory deprivation. "My beloved son was left with the severest form of sensory deprivation," she states emphatically. "Physical murder and death!"

On the surface it can appear that the parents have become hard-hearted and judgmental. Nothing could be further from the truth. What appears to be hard-heartedness and a quickness to judge are expressions of their anger. The parents have been robbed of their child and of their propensity to trust. They believed that most humans are inherently good. They shared that belief with their child and their child was murdered. The murderer is still alive and someday will probably be set free to resume his or her life. "My son is buried in the ground," continues Mary. "There is no life for this wonderful, talented, productive, contributing member of society."

In 1993, Sandra's young adult daughter died after being shot in the face with a .357 Magnum. The daughter's boyfriend was the person who pulled the trigger. "He wanted to do drugs," Sandra explains, "and my daughter didn't want him to so they began to argue."

Sandra proudly describes her family as a blended family. It consists of her three children, her husband's two children, and three adopted children. By adopting three children, Sandra has proven herself to be a person who cares about and helps other people. "My daughter was like me," she says. "She thought she could *help* her boyfriend stay off drugs."

Because Sandra and her daughter spent their lives helping others, she is angry that her daughter was murdered by a man she tried to help. "I feel anger rise up in me at the oddest times," she explains. "Like when I saw two men fighting in a public store and I stepped between them to break it up. I am only 5′ tall and usually non-assertive. I was so angry that they were getting violent-sounding and could hurt someone."

Living with anger is another negative change the parents must endure. As Sandra explained, it can erupt at any time. After her anger erupted and she stepped in between the two men who were fighting, she wondered what could have happened to her if one of them had had a gun. She learned that her anger has the potential of placing her in physical danger.

Damaged Relationships

The parents' anger is potentially dangerous in other ways as well. It can damage relationships they share with others—including their own marriage. The mother of a murdered child recently told me that her marriage of thirty-three years had gone down hill. To explain this down hill slide, she said that her husband thinks she should be able to put her grief and her anger behind her. If this bereaved mother could dispose of these negative emotions, her life would be so much easier, and she is striving to do so. However, at the same time, her grief is made more complex by her inability to understand why her husband has been able to work through his grief while she has not.

Mata can empathize with this grieving mother. "My husband and I had a fairly good marriage," she says, "but when our daughter was murdered our lives fell apart. The only reason I stayed was because I took my daughter's two sons to raise. I felt they needed me."

The breakup of their marriage is perhaps the most detrimental change the parents must endure. Before the murder, they and their child were a complete family. Their love was an unbroken circle. When their child died, a segment was ripped out of that circle. When they divorced, it was broken in two.

Anyone who is divorced, or in the process of getting a divorce, knows firsthand the havoc a divorce can create. It brings with it its own form of grief. It forces the man and the woman to establish new lives. When those seeking the divorce are the parents of a murdered child, the devastation they feel is two-fold. They have withstood one agonizing loss and now they must withstand another. They have been struggling to establish new lives and now, because the divorce tears their new lives in two, they must begin the process all over again. The agony and anguish they feel increase to an almost unbearable level as do their feelings of loneliness and isolation. It is a miracle they manage to survive these combined tragedies.

POSITIVE CHANGES

After the parents are no longer distracted by the investigation, the trial, and the sentencing, they start to feel the full impact of their grief. As they progress through the grieving process they become increasingly aware that their lives have been hideously changed. But, at the same time, they are amazed to discover that these hideous changes are off-set, in part, by positive changes. The parents become confused. They, and all who know them, struggle to comprehend how and why a child's murder can bring about a modicum of edifying change.

Enhanced Awareness of the Value of Life

Evelyn comments that since the dark day her daughter was stabbed to death, both she and her life have changed completely. Overall, these changes have been detrimental—with one significant exception. "I now love life much more," she says.

You might ask how the parents of a murdered child can profess to love life more when they obviously despise the absence of their child and the excruciating pain this absence causes. Jenny explains this seemingly contradictory statement. "I now know how fragile life is," she says, "and that each day must be lived to the fullest." As all of us know a life that is lived to the fullest is a life to be treasured. And who among us does not love what we treasure?

Freedom from Some Worries

In a way that might, at first, seem strange to the grieving parents, and to all who come in contact with them, the murder of a child makes some aspects of the parents' lives a little easier. Because they have suffered the ultimate tragedy—the death of their child—they now view many of life's problems as minor rather than major. "I look at things that used to be absolutely unbelievable situations," says Evelyn, "as now, much more bearable."

Jenny agrees with Evelyn. "Things which used to stress me—being stuck in traffic, money worries, job security—no longer irritate me," she says. "If I find myself in one of those situations I think to myself: *if this is the worst thing that happens to me today I am having a pretty good day."*

Increased Value of Loved Ones

Many parents state that the murder of their child jolted them awake to the realization that the people who share their day-to-day lives are very valuable. They were also awakened to the importance of letting those people know how much they are loved. "I always finish a conversation with 'I am so glad we are friends.' or 'I really love you.' " continues Jenny. "You just never know if you will have the chance to say those things again."

Mary expresses the same thought in a slightly different way. "My immediate family now comes first," she states firmly.

When a child is murdered the parents often become more protective of each other and of their living children. This protective attitude can be positive. It can weld the remaining family members into a solid unit of love and caring.

A Heightened Sense of Compassion

The devastation the parents have suffered clears their vision and hones their instincts. They don't need to see overt evidence of another person's troubles. They sense sadness and turmoil and respond accordingly. Carolyn finds that she now has an enormous sense of compassion. "The feelings of love and compassion for others whose child has been murdered are overwhelming," she says. "I want to do anything that might help someone else get through a similar experience."

When Carolyn's son was shot to death outside of a bus station, both he and Carolyn became the victims of a homicide. But the compassion that she and parents like her feel is not limited only to other victims. It branches out into their families and communities like the roots of a tree. Like Carolyn, Jenny has found that she is much more compassionate. "And," she says, "I am also a better listener."

Strengthened Personality Traits

In addition to a heightened sense of compassion and an elevated awareness of the value they place on the people who share their lives, the parents soon discover that they have changed in other positive ways as well. Deena says that before her son was murdered she was rather wishy-washy. "Since becoming serious about 'recovering' from the ordeal of my son's death, I have become more assertive," she says. "I want to do anything I can to help the rights of children and of parents whose children have been murdered."

Evelyn has found that she is more tenacious and strong-willed. "I would go above and beyond now for a cause when I wouldn't have before," she says. "People don't realize. It can happen to them."

* * *

While it can be satisfying for the parents to use the few positive changes in their lives to enhance and enrich the lives of others, their satisfaction is permanently sullied by their child's absence.

Since my daughter was murdered, I have become more sensitive to the needs of my family, friends, neighbors, and co-workers. When I look at myself in the mirror, I can see the lingering sadness in my eyes. Because I can see my own sadness, I can easily discern the sadness in the eyes of others. While my new-found sensitivity pleases me, I must admit that I would prefer having the pleasure of my daughter still being alive. The endless longing I feel to have her with me again conflicts with the pleasure I feel at having become a more compassionate person.

Most parents of a murdered child have difficulty learning to live with these conflicting feelings. Like a tennis ball being lobbed back and forth, they are first batted forward by their heightened sense of compassion and then batted back by their grief. Because they experience conflicting feelings, they send mixed signals to the people who interact with them. These people, unless they have suffered a similar loss or are very tuned in to the parents' feelings of grief, can find it difficult to interpret and deal with the mixed signals they send. For instance, on a day when the parents have had the satisfaction of helping someone solve a personal problem, they might appear to be a little less grief-stricken than they were the day before. Family members, friends, and others mistakenly interpret the parents' satisfaction as an easing of their grief. They begin to believe that the parents have begun to heal and they breathe a sigh of relief. What they do not know is that the parents' satisfaction is temporary. When grief floods back in the following day, they are baffled. Why, they wonder, did they think that the parents were beginning to heal when they obviously are not?

The answer is relatively simple. Larry explains that the violence of his son's execution-style murder was like an earthquake. "I believe I will have aftershocks for the rest of my life," he says. These aftershocks are actually the many ways in which the parents' lives have been permanently and detrimentally changed.

When you think back on the statements made by Jenny, Pam, Deena, Evelyn, Mary, Carolyn, Christina, Filiberto, Carol, Chet, Patricia, Beckie, Sandra, and Mata you need to remember that they are not fictional characters. They are flesh and blood people who never dreamed they would become the victims of a homicide. Their tears and their agonies are very real.

And, when you think back on the statements made by these parents, you might ask if it is possible for you to help the parents of a murdered child to survive their grief. The answer is yes. If you are strong and patient, and if you listen with an open mind to what is in their hearts and are sensitive to their needs, you definitely can.

CHAPTER 6

Immediate Help You Can Give the Parents of a Murdered Child

How do you pick out burial clothes for your daughter?

Jenny
1-12-93

Above all else, when someone is dealing with a grieving parent, they should simply be there. Their physical presence isn't always needed but their emotional one is. Just by knowing that someone out there cares can be a great comfort, especially when everything out there looks a million times scarier than it once did.

Deena
1-22-96

Now that you know the emotions of murdered-child grief, the parents' difficulties in dealing with the criminal justice system, and the many permanent changes that occur in their lives, you can see why this type of grief is so devastating and complex. It can take years for the grieving parents to fully understand its intricate tangle of ruinous emotions. Until they are able to interpret their grief, it will be hard for them to explain their feelings to family members, friends, and others.

In the beginning, the parents' minds are filled to capacity with the horror of their child's murder. Despite this, they must deal with the police, the medical examiner, and possibly the media. They must also perform necessary tasks such as notifying loved ones, preparing for the funeral, continuing to take care of their living children, and maintaining their home—just to name a few. Obviously it is not possible for the parents to do it all alone. In some cases they cannot depend on receiving help from members of their immediate families because they, too, are stunned and horrified by the child's murder.

The parents will need help from the moment their child dies and well into the future. Giving them that help is not going to be easy for anyone associated with them. But it can be done. Help can come in many different forms and from a variety of sources. You are one of these sources.

OFFER IMMEDIATE AND SPECIFIC HELP

If you are close to one or both of the parents, either personally or professionally, visit them in their home to offer help. The length of your visit will be determined by the relationship you share with them and by how many people are already there. Handled properly, your visit will not be intrusive and you will not be in the way. Considering the crisis state the parents and their immediate families are in, a few cool heads will be desperately needed. This does not mean that you should attempt to take control but, if the parents are floundering in a sea of confusion and hectic activity, there are ways you can rescue them.

A death produces many incoming and outgoing phone calls. When the cause of death is murder, the number of calls increase considerably and the parents can need someone to help man their phone. Because an autopsy is usually performed, there can be a delay of several days before the child's body is ready for viewing and burial. During this time, many people, including members of the press, might visit the parents. Someone will also be needed to help greet these people, or even to act as a liaison or spokesperson. When you arrive at their home, you might be asked to assume one of these responsibilities so take a pad of paper and a pen with you. You will want to keep an accurate record of who came to the house, who phoned, and of all messages received.

The parents will need help in other ways as well. As they are not thinking clearly, your offer to help must be specific rather than vague. Because you, too, have been affected by the murder, you might need to organize your thoughts by making a list of tasks that would need doing if a member of your household died, plus a week of your daily responsibilities.

After your list is complete, you can decide which tasks you are able to do for the parents. For example, you can offer to provide care for young or aged members of the family, arrange transportation and lodging for out-of-state relatives, feed the family pet, do the laundry, dust the furniture, mow the lawn, or wash the car they will be using to attend the viewings. On the morning of my daughter's funeral, my sister-in-law, a hairstylist, came to my house and shampooed and curled my hair. Her kind act helped guide me through the task of getting ready for the most sorrow-filled day of my life, and helped preserve what little energy I had to deal with the trauma of burying my child. More importantly, having her with me was a great comfort. Her physical presence made me aware that she shared my pain.

You can also offer to drive the parents to see their priest, minister, rabbi or other cleric, or to the flower shop, or to see the funeral director. "My three best friends helped with funeral arrangements and they went with me to the viewing," states Jenny. "They did other things I could not do because I was in a state of shock."

After deciding which tasks best suit your relationship with the parents, your abilities, and the amount of time you have to give, write them down on a piece of paper along with your name and phone number. If the parents are not at home when you visit, or, for some reason, are not available to speak with you, leave the paper with the person who is greeting visitors, a family member, or a neighbor.

Although you definitely are not required to take the parents a gift, you might want to prepare a healthy snack or beverage they can share with other visitors, a main dish casserole they can use immediately or store in their freezer for future use, or put together an assortment of disposable plates, cutlery, and napkins. Bringing one of these three gifts serves two purposes. First, it relieves the parents of the need to wash dishes, shop for groceries, and cook meals during the dark days prior to and after the funeral. Second, because this visit might be the most stressful you have ever had to make, it can be made easier by saying, "I just stopped by to drop this off and to offer my sympathy."

Rest assured that many grieving parents will be aware of your distress. When Elsie's daughter was stabbed to death, she found that most people she encountered were afraid of the word murder. "Afraid that if this terrible thing could happen to their friends," she explains, "it could also happen to them." If you are frightened by the word murder, and most of us are, think about the terrible emotional state the parents are in and you will be able to put your fear aside.

While you are in the parents' home, do not be hurt if they are not available to speak with you. Certain responsibilities associated with the police investigation and the funeral are their's alone. They might be away from home tending to these responsibilities or handling them by phone. Also, even though they are in shock, the parents are struggling to cope with their excruciating pain. They might be resting or simply incapable of speaking with anyone.

Do not be hurt if the parents do not take you up on your offer to help. The offer itself is extremely valuable. Later, when their faith in the goodness of mankind and trust in the world begin to slip away, they will remember your visit and not feel so betrayed and alone.

If you don't have time to visit the parents, do not think there is nothing you can do to help. Be aware that they are dreading the ordeal of the funeral as well as the moment when they will be left alone with their grief. These dreads can be less ominous if they know that other mourners are not going to leave them abruptly. "The day of my daughter's funeral and the following day, many friends and family stayed with us to bring us comfort," Jenny comments gratefully.

You can begin planning a buffet breakfast or luncheon to be served after the funeral in the parents' home, a room in their church, or in your home. The food and drink served need not be expensive or elaborate. If you are not able to handle hosting such a meal by yourself, either physically or financially, you can ask other friends of the family to bring a covered dish, a dessert, a beverage, paper goods, or flowers to brighten the buffet table. Most people will pitch in willingly. And they will help you serve and clean up afterward.

Or you can gather the names of people willing to share the responsibility of phoning the parents once a day for several weeks after the funeral. When contact is made, the caller can say something like, "I wanted to let you know that I was thinking about you, and to ask if there is anything I can do for you." These phone calls will not be easy to make. More than likely the parents will want to voice their pain, and the group of people you have organized to keep tabs on them will need to know that they must be prepared to listen calmly and patiently.

DO NOT PROBE FOR DETAILS OF THE MURDER

If you do have the opportunity to see the parents while you are visiting their home, please do not ask questions about the murder. Some might view your questions as morbid curiosity rather than genuine sympathy, and be deeply hurt.

Others, however, will begin telling you the details the minute they see you. They need to repeat them over and over again because the murder seems so unreal to them. This can be traumatic for you and it can pose a dilemma. You will want to acknowledge the parents' disbelief and horror, but, if you are shocked by the way in which their child was murdered, you do not want to draw away from them either emotionally or physically. If you cannot think of an appropriate verbal response, you might gently touch their hand or arm. Many grieving parents need to feel the touch of a sympathetic person more than they need to hear a sympathetic voice. If you feel comfortable giving the parents a hug, do so. "One of the best things I think could help is a hug," says Deena. "The one thing I wanted the most was for someone to hold me."

If you are the parent of a murdered child, contact the parents immediately. If you are not, but are acquainted with the parent of a murdered child, or know of a support group for parents of murdered children, phone that parent or a member of that support group and ask if they will contact the parents. Pam explains, "I can still remember how I felt that Friday night four years ago," she says. "All I wanted to do was to talk to someone that had lost a child to murder. Someone that I could talk to just to hear them say, 'I know how you feel.' Someone that I could look at and know that I, too, would survive."

HONOR THE CHILD'S MEMORY

Prior to attending the viewings, many people send flowers or some other tribute to the funeral home. These types of tributes are always appropriate and will be deeply appreciated. But you should contact the funeral director before making your purchase to determine if the parents would prefer that a donation be made to a specific group or organization in lieu of flowers.

One of the parents' greatest fears is that other people will eventually forget their child. The old adage "out of sight, out of mind" runs through their heads. Considering this, you might choose to send something more lasting than flowers. Most children have a special talent or interest. For example, Filiberto's daughter loved acting and took drama classes in school. While Christina's family lived in Japan, her daughter studied art. Sandra's daughter was a gifted clothing designer. Coaching little league teams was one of the many pastimes Carol's son enjoyed. Pam's daughter played softball and was a cheerleader. If the murdered child had a particular interest, you can make a donation of money or time in the child's name to an individual or group participating in the same interest. Or you can set up a scholarship or award fund. Mary's son wrote poetry and music and was interested in the media. After his death, his peers established an award that is given annually to a young student in one of these fields. Mary is very proud that her son's name lives on through this award and that deserving youths are receiving help because of him.

If you have access to a poem, a song, a piece of art work, or some other object the child created or treasured, you might want to have it permanently preserved in some way so that you can present it to the parents. For instance, you can have the poem or song reproduced on parchment paper by a skilled calligraphist, or purchase a wooden base and glass dome to hold the child's favorite baseball, doll, or some other treasure.

Planning and preparing a permanent tribute can take several days or weeks. If your tribute is not ready to be presented to the parents during one of the viewings or the funeral, make them aware of it in a handwritten note. They will be touched and grateful that you took the time to honor their child in such a unique and meaningful way and that you, too, were aware of their child's special interest or talent.

There are also other lasting tributes you can send. These include shrubs and trees the parents can plant in their yard, or in the cemetery if this is permitted. Or, if one or both of the parents have a green thumb, you can purchase a houseplant for them to nurture and watch grow. "I brought plants home from the cemetery and planted a garden in memory of my daughter," says Sandra. "It is a special rock garden and in it are planted love and memories from her friends and loved ones."

You can also place a photograph of the deceased child in a unique frame that matches the parents' decor, or have the photograph reproduced as a pen-and-ink drawing or oil painting.

Do not wrap your tribute in brightly colored paper and ribbons. The parents are not feeling festive, and you do not want them to think that you are trivializing their grief.

ATTEND THE VIEWINGS AND THE FUNERAL

Attending the funeral home viewings is also going to be traumatic. As you approach the funeral home door, your heart will be pounding and you will be asking yourself, *What am I going to say?* Keep in mind that it is better to say too little than too much. Jenny was helped when her friends acknowledged that they didn't know the pain she was feeling. "They also said that they couldn't take away the pain," she says, "and that they were sorry my daughter was murdered." If you don't know what to say you might, again, opt for holding the parents' hands, or giving them a gentle hug.

While you are in the funeral home, remember that the parents will miss their child for the remainder of their lives. This will prevent you from making a statement inferring that, instead of being sad, they should be grateful for having had their child for X number of years. Remember also that the parents created their child and that the relationship they shared was the most important one in their lives. Having their creation brutally beaten, stabbed, or shot to death causes pain that only another parent of a murdered child can fully comprehend. "I have buried several people in my lifetime," explains Deena, "and while it was painful to lose those precious people, I never experienced the same kind of pain as when my son was murdered. The grief the parents feel is so different from any other pain known to man. It is a very physical pain as well as emotional.

"And," she continues, "don't say, 'At least you have other children.' I love my children but none of them are my son and I haven't expected them to be him. Other children in the home may keep the parents going but they don't stop the pain. On top of that, the parents have to worry about dealing with the siblings' grief over the loss. No matter how much children fight, they all suffer when one is taken."

The parents realize that no one would intentionally say something hurtful. But, all too often, because the murder of a child causes severe stress for all who come in contact with them, a hurtful statement can inadvertently slip out. You might be less nervous if you key in on the fact that the parents don't know what to say to you either. Life did not prepare them to be the parents of a murdered child any more than it prepared you to give support in this most horrible of situations.

It is always appropriate to say something that lets the parents know you thought their child was beautiful or handsome, or a pleasure to know, or that you recognized a talent or special personality trait the child possessed. If you were not acquainted with their child, don't be afraid to admit it. You can say something like, "I'm sorry that I didn't know your daughter. What was she like?" or "I'm sorry that I didn't know your son very well. What were some of the things he liked to do?" All parents enjoy talking about their children and bereaved parents are no exception. And, because the parents are struggling to erase the brutality of their child's murder from their minds, they will be grateful for the opportunity to talk about their child in a positive way.

The horror of being notified of the murder is second only to the horror of the funeral. Seeing their child's body lowered into the ground, or placed in a vault, slams home the cruel reality that the parents will never again hug, kiss, or speak with their child. You can help them get through this traumatic time by again honoring the memory of their child. If you knew the child well, and if you feel comfortable speaking in public, you can ask to give a short eulogy. Or, as in Jenny's case, you might give an impromptu eulogy. "Not only did the minister speak," explains Jenny, "but family members and my daughter's friends were also given the opportunity to pay her oral tribute. This was not planned so it was very touching to hear these affirmations given spontaneously and from the heart."

HELP WITH FUNERAL RELATED TASKS

When a child, teenager, or young adult dies, many people express their sympathy in a wide variety of ways. A month or so after the funeral, the parents will want to acknowledge these kind acts by writing and mailing out thank you notes specifically acknowledging the individual gift or action of the person to whom it is addressed. Due to the parents' pain and exhaustion, preparing to write these notes can overwhelm them and it can take several months for them to begin. You can help by making a list of people to whom notes need to be written. This list should contain the recipients full names and addresses as well as the gift or action being acknowledged. Or you can offer to purchase a quantity of note paper or cards, and postage stamps. If your tastes are similar to those of the parents, you can make the actual purchase and present it to them as a gift. You can also prepare a general outline that can be altered slightly for each note, and offer to come to the parents' home to help write the notes. Even if you don't do any of the actual writing, you can help keep them on track by gently reminding them of the task at hand. And you can ensure that they have the time to write the notes by doing some of their household chores for them.

If you chose to honor the memory of their child by purchasing a shrub or tree to be planted in the parents' yard or at the cemetery, it would be most beneficial if you offered to help with the planting. Before making your purchase, ask the parents what type of plant they prefer. If the plant is to be placed in the cemetery, check with cemetery personnel to determine if the plant selected is appropriate. Arrange a planting date that is convenient for both you and the parents, and have the florist or nursery deliver the plant to the proper location on that date. Remember to bring shovels, gardening gloves, fertilizer, mulch, or whatever else the florist or nursery person tells you is necessary, plus instructions on how to care for the plant in the future. You can also bring a hot or cold drink, depending on the weather, and a light snack to be eaten after the planting. Although this will not be a happy occasion for the parents, offering them something to eat and drink will allow a few minutes of rest during which you might reminisce about their child.

DO NOT ASSESS BLAME OR ALLOW THE PARENTS TO BLAME THEMSELVES

When a child is murdered, some parents ask *why* this tragedy happened to them. Unfortunately, because they are in a state of shock and disbelief, they might attempt to answer this question by blaming themselves for allowing it to happen. "I had to deal with the fact that I hadn't been there to protect my son," says Deena. "I didn't need others blaming me for not being there for him at the moment of his death."

If the grieving parents blame themselves, you can help them by firmly, but gently, pointing out that parents cannot protect their children twenty-four hours a day, and that some people, even those who are close to us, are capable of appearing to be trustworthy when they are not.

The parents' relatives are also struggling to determine the *why* of the murder. And, because of their shock and disbelief, they might also attempt to answer this question by unthinkingly making statements that suggest that the parents are to blame. After my daughter was murdered, I spoke with parents whose families told them that their murdered child should not have been allowed to associate with the wrong kind of people, or that they should not have been allowed to go to an unfamiliar place. When the words *an unfamiliar place* were used, some of these parents interpreted them to mean *an unsafe place.* Mary's eighteen-year-old son, who was extremely intelligent and had bright hopes and many plans for his future, left the familiarity of his East coast hometown to explore educational and employment opportunities in a large California city. When relatives inferred that he might be to blame for his death because he had left his *familiar* hometown to go to an *unfamiliar* city, Mary angrily responded, "It was his right to a safe environment."

When a child is murdered while pursuing his or her inalienable right to life, liberty, and the pursuit of happiness, the parents are enraged. Inferring that pursuing this right caused their child's death, increases their pain and deepens their despair.

And they should not be told that the murder occurred because their child just happened to be in the wrong place at the wrong time. This subtly infers that the murder was accidental rather than intentional. It does not assuage the parents' rage. It enhances it.

Some parents believe that their friends and relatives attempt to determine the cause of the murder because they are afraid that their child will be murdered. All parents have a difficult time molding their children into well-rounded individuals. Most of the time they feel like acrobats balancing on a tightrope. They must somehow teach their children to be cautious and safety conscious while, at the same time, allowing them sufficient freedom to learn to detect potentially dangerous situations. When Christina's daughter was raped, beaten, and run over by a car, one of Christina's friends blatantly blamed her for the murder. "She said that I was to blame because I had been too protective of my three girls," says Christina. "She then said that, because I was too strict with my daughters, I deserved this."

You might be shocked that Christina was told something so cruel and hurtful. But, because some parents fear for the safety of their own children, they allow their fear to supersede logic and they speak without thinking.

DO NOT TURN YOUR BACK ON THE PARENTS

There have been cases where a close family member avoided contact with the parents from the minute they learned of the child's murder. Several years ago, a grieving father told me that his son's step-grandmother seemed to be extremely embarrassed by the murder. "She tried to stay at arm's length," he explained. "At the funeral, she refused to ride in the family car or to sit with the family during the service. This ostracism has continued."

There have also been cases where family members refused to speak about the child or the murder. More recently I was told by a grieving mother that her mother-in-law shows her no concern and does not ask questions about how the police investigation is progressing. In fact, if the mother mentions the investigation, her mother-in-law tells her to forget it because the police are never going to find out anything. Another mother told me that, although she knows that her sister truly cares, she never allows her to talk about her murdered son or the murder.

When a child has been murdered the parents feel as if they have been shot out of a cannon and are hurtling through space. They want to come back to earth but, without the support of everyone connected to them, it is difficult for them to do so. The parents need to feel the touch of other people—people who are not afraid to let them cry on their shoulder or to cry with them. Evelyn states that she has been helped by the man she was in love with in 1984, the year her daughter was murdered. "I married him a year or so afterward," she says. "From notification to this day he has stood by me. He helps just by holding me when I need it."

Deena also credits the man she married several years ago with helping her survive the ordeal of her son's murder. "He held me and let me cry when I needed to cry," she says. "That was the one thing I wanted the most. It is something I wish someone had done a whole lot sooner."

The support of family members is crucial to the parents' survival. In 1992 Janetta's thirty-year-old son died after a 9-millimeter, hollow-point bullet tore through his chest. He and a friend were driving in the friend's car to a convenience store when they made a wrong turn and encountered a gang fight. When the police twice came to Janetta's home after the shooting, they told her only that her son had been in a fight. Hours later, after her son's best friend informed her that a neighbor had told him that her son had been shot, Janetta phoned the police, hospitals in her area, and the morgue and eventually learned that her son was dead. She was enraged, as would be any parent, that the police had not immediately informed her of her son's death. Since the shooting, Janetta's daughters have given her the support she needs to survive her grief and her rage. "My four girls have been there for me," she says, "And they continue to be by my side."

Before her son was gunned down on the street, Beckie's family consisted of her and her husband, their son and daughter. When the family became homicide victims, the three remaining members learned to support one another. "As a family we have picked each other up when we've fallen," explains Beckie.

The support of friends is also vitally important to the parents' survival. Filiberto explains that his wife, Helga, has three female friends who have stood by her since their daughter was strangled to death. "They are all helpful," he says. "They comfort her when she is depressed."

Friends of the murdered child can also help the parents. Young people sometimes express their grief freely; they tend to be less stoic and are not ashamed to cry. After Janetta's son was shot to death, his friends frequently came to visit her. "They were very supportive," she says.

In August of 1994, Joan's thirty-eight-year-old son was shot in the back with a shotgun held at close range. "He was at a friend's apartment," she says, "and the friend shot him. The friend said it was an accident but neither the police nor the family believe it. We think that he wanted to control my son. We accepted a plea bargain because there were no witnesses and the District Attorney convinced us that, in our county, the shooter would be believed. If he didn't get a guilty verdict, he would serve only one year or less."

Accepting a plea bargain, and knowing that their child's killer is going to receive a reduced sentence, further traumatizes and devastates the parents. Joan explains that she has survived this added trauma because she has a very close friend who, because she suffers the pain of crippling arthritis, can relate to Joan's pain. "We've talked and prayed together on a regular basis," says Joan. "After my son died, she called me every weekday and just checked on me. Sometimes we talked a little, sometimes a lot. Sometimes we cried. We get together for a couple of hours about once a month. With her I can say anything I feel no matter how weird it sounds and she never thinks I am nuts."

CONTINUE TO OFFER PHYSICAL HELP

When a child is murdered, the parents' lives become a nightmare of anguish, confusion, and hectic activity. The agony they feel weighs them down like a two-ton barbell. Carrying this weight they stumble blindly through the maze of the criminal justice system. Meanwhile, life goes on and they struggle to keep up with their responsibilities at home and at work.

For several months, and sometimes until the trial and sentencing are over, the parents will need your help to lighten the burden they carry. You can offer to do many things for them, such as dropping clothes off at the dry cleaners, cooking them a meal, cleaning their house, or watching their children while they are meeting with the police or the prosecuting attorney. Deena advises, "Rather than say to the parents, 'If there's anything I can do . . .' give them your phone number and tell them to call any time, day or night."

It can never be said often enough that all parents respond to the murder of their child differently, and that all parents, depending on a variety of factors including their individual personalities, grieve differently. The parent with whom you come in contact might naturally be outgoing or bold, and might easily ask for your help. Or that parent might be shy or reserved and will find that asking for help is difficult. Due to these differences, you might consider taking Deena's advice one step further by staying alert for specific areas in which the parents need help and then specifically offering that help. Tell them you will be at their house on Saturday at 10:00 A.M. to pick up their grocery list or to take their dog to the veterinarian, or at 2:00 P.M. to rake and bag the leaves in their yard.

Some parents will hire a private investigator if the police have been unable to solve the case. Others will need the advice of an attorney or an accountant to help settle their child's estate. Because the parents are in shock and excruciating pain, they are vulnerable to shysters who earn their living preying on the confusion and misfortunes of others. Two years ago I spoke with a couple whose young adult daughter was shot to death in 1990. These parents, both in their late sixties, told me that the police had ruled the death a suicide. They, however, were certain that their daughter had been murdered, and that they knew who the murderer was. In an effort to prove murder, they had over the course of the years, hired several attorneys and private investigators to look into the case. Each of these persons turned out to be unreliable, and eventually the couple lost their home to bankruptcy. These bad experiences compounded their grief, and left them bitter and disillusioned. While many families do have a reliable family attorney to advise them on day-to-day issues such as drawing up a will, few ever have the need to hire an attorney who specializes in criminal law, or a private investigator. If the parents you are attempting to help have never before used such services, and you know of a reliable professional, give them that person's name and phone number, or offer to make an appointment for them. You can also offer to drive them to see this person. But do not plan on sitting in on the meeting unless the parents request your presence.

CONTINUE TO OFFER EMOTIONAL SUPPORT

One of the main reasons the parents of a murdered child join a support group is so they can openly express their feelings of grief and horror. This does not mean, however, that they do not need additional support from their family, friends, and others. Jenny has found that her three best friends have helped her immensely. "They have spent hours on the phone with me at all hours of the night listening to me when I was having a very *hard* day," states Jenny. "They do not tell me to put my daughter's death behind me, or to get on with my life, or that she is in a better place, or to be strong. They let me be however I need to be."

Chet is grateful to a female co-worker whom, he says, "helped me preserve my sanity. She and her family gave me love and support. She was there when I needed her, but she didn't waste time with syrupy sympathy. By pushing, threatening, and being firm, she forced me to do the things I needed to do."

Although some parents would not appreciate this level of firmness, many do need guidance. If you take the time to learn how to read their moods, and listen with your heart to what they are saying, you will know how to help them.

A friend of Sandra's, because she listened to Sandra and was astute to her needs, gave her a popular book dealing with life after death. "I read the book to my husband," comments Sandra, "and we discussed it. It helped us a lot."

Before you give or recommend a book to the parents, you should be as familiar with its content as you are with them. If the book is not compatible with their needs, it can hurt rather than help them.

Do not automatically assume that the parents will appreciate receiving a religious book even though they are religious. Keep in mind that the parents want nothing more than to have their child back with them. Some parents will not want to be told that their child is in a better place. They will question why God took their child away from them. They will wonder why God allowed their child to be brutally murdered and will temporarily, or perhaps permanently, reject their faith. Other parents will accept the murder as God's will and depend on their faith to see them through. To help her survive her daughter's murder, Sandra relied on her faith. "Without the gospel of Jesus Christ," she says, "I don't know what I would have done. Having that stability is second nature to me."

* * *

Before offering to help the parents, take a step back to assess their needs. Because they are floundering and confused, they might be sending mixed signals and you will be forced to make educated guesses as to the most appropriate ways to help them. This will probably result in a misjudgment or two. But as the parents begin to think more clearly they will forgive these errors in judgment. They will realize that you did the best you could; that you were sincerely and courageously trying to help. They will appreciate that you cared enough to reach out your hand to them.

As time passes you will become more skilled at determining the most appropriate ways to help. You will be a valuable source of help and support in the future.

CHAPTER 7

Future Help You Can Give the Parents of a Murdered Child

> Being a single parent, and raising my son and four girls alone, my support has always been, since my son was murdered, my girls. They have been there for me, and they will continue to be by my side.
>
> *Janetta*
> *3-20-96*

> My insides felt as if they were going to explode. I just wanted to scream at the top of my lungs, "Why me? Why was my daughter taken from me?" I talk about this a great deal in our support group meetings.
>
> *Pam*
> *3-12-96*

To successfully complete the grieving process, the parents of a murdered child are going to need help for many years from everyone with whom they come in contact. The help you give can range from small acts of kindness that occur sporadically to being actively supportive on a regular and ongoing basis. For example, you can, with little effort, treat them the same way you always have whenever you happen to encounter them. Or, although you might find it much more difficult, you can give them opportunities to talk about the murder for as long as they need to.

While determining the most appropriate ways to help the parents, keep in mind that their futures hold agony and anguish, exhaustion and terror, uncertainty and resentment. During the first few years they can be driven to thoughts of suicide to end their unbearable pain. Also keep in mind that, depending on whether the murder is unsolved or solved, and on the outcome of the trial and the sentencing, they can be filled with rage.

I do not want what I have just written to make you feel powerless to help the parents, or to instill such a feeling of dread that you do an abrupt about-face and hurry away every time you see them approaching. But I do want you to know that helping them will often require patience and determination. While progressing through grief, they will experience mood swings. One minute, because their pain has eased temporarily, they will optimistically believe they are conquering their grief. The next minute, when a poignant reminder stimulates and increases their pain, they will become despondent. They will wonder if their grief is going to last forever and how they are going to survive if it does.

In the course of helping the parents you will experience similar, and equally frustrating, feelings. As you witness their optimism change to despondency, you will wonder if your efforts are doing them any good at all and if you are working in vain. When this happens, tell yourself that you *are* helping them. Continue to forge ahead, and at some point in the future, you will clearly begin to see the fruits of your labor.

TREAT THEM AS YOU ALWAYS HAVE

It is extremely helpful for the parents to know that the people with whom they interact on a daily or weekly basis, such as their co-workers, their living children's teachers, cashiers at the grocery store, their hairstylist or barber, their mail carrier, and others, are not uncomfortable in their presence. The parents realize that the horror of a child, teenager, or young adult being murdered is the reason why some people show discomfort, and they try to accept it. But, even so, when they are faced with the discomfort of others, they are hurt. It is also helpful for the parents to know that no one is going to make them feel uncomfortable because they have become the victims of a repulsive act of brutality. You can prevent this be treating them as you always have. This does not mean that you are going to ignore their situation or their grief. If you did not see them prior to, or during the funeral, acknowledge their child's murder by expressing your sympathy the first time you do see them. The murder of a child, teenager, or young adult stirs feelings of shock and sorrow in all of us whether or not we are acquainted with the parents. We know that the child's life was brutally cut short for no rhyme or reason, and that the parents have been cruelly deprived of their dearest treasure. Prior to their child's murder, the parents felt that same shock and sorrow when they heard that someone else's child had been murdered. Because they have felt the same shock and sorrow that you are feeling now, a simple statement such as, "I was sorry to hear of your daughter's (or son's) death," can be the most appropriate expression of sympathy for you to make.

Expressing your sympathy is beneficial in two important ways. Once the subject is out in the open it will be easier for you to treat the parents as you always have. And, because they will then know that their relationship with you is not going to change, they will not shy away from you. The security of being able to frequent places and to be involved in situations that are familiar to them is invaluable. It can make their lives a little easier.

DO NOT EXPECT TOO MUCH TOO QUICKLY

As stated previously murdered-child grief is extremely complex. The emotional pain caused by the parents' negative feelings is a constant burden. Carrying it around causes a physical pain that can be compared to the nagging and sometimes severe ache one develops after exercising too strenuously or lifting too heavy an object—only this ache does not go away in a few days. When their emotional pain is combined with this physical pain, the parents become exhausted. "It's all they can do to get out of bed in the morning," states Deena.

Day after day the parents force their bodies and their minds to function, and they yearn for one good night of solid sleep. But that, too, is denied them. Because of the many thoughts that careen through their heads, they have trouble falling asleep, and when they do, they often have nightmares.

In an attempt to maintain some shred of normalcy, and to give themselves something else to think about, most parents return to work almost immediately. "Unfortunately," Deena continues, "they don't do well. It's hard to think with all those emotions running rampant in your head." If you supervise or work with one of the parents, you can help by not expecting them to perform at peak capacity for quite some time. You can also help by tactfully overseeing or assuming part of their workload, and by willingly and graciously honoring their requests for time off to take care of matters associated with the investigation and the trial.

Some parents also resume participating in pastime activities as well as taking on additional activities. They are determined that their child's killer will not rob them of everything they hold dear, and they need to keep busy. Trying to take their minds off of their grief by indulging in too many activities adds to their exhaustion. If you participate in a leisure or community activity with one or both of the parents, you might have to pick up the slack their lack of concentration causes. A friend of mine whose son was killed in a car accident a year and a half ago sings in her church choir. Since her son's death, certain hymns cause her to break down and she begins to cry. Rather than withdraw from the choir, which helps to keep her focused on life rather than death, she is sticking it out. But, she told me, she could not do this without the help of the other choir members. They cover for her by singing louder. And they never act embarrassed or uncomfortable.

For several months, and perhaps even longer, helping the parents in these ways will place an extra burden on you. But it will keep them connected to places and activities that are stable and unchanging. With the many traumatic and permanent changes that have occurred in their lives they need stability in order to survive.

When you are with the parents do not turn away if they mention their child, the investigation, or the trial. Filiberto is very grateful because the people with whom he works have remained supportive during the years since his daughter was strangled. "They are still sympathetic," he says.

For several weeks or months after the child's murder, the parents will, at times, deny reality. They might fantasize that a bizarre mistake has been made. Somehow, they buried someone else's child; somewhere their child is alive and well. This type of behavior is not abnormal. It is merely a manifestation of the parents' burning and constant desire to have their child with them again. When their pain threatens to break them emotionally, they save themselves, so to speak, by conjuring up these types of fantasies. If they express their fantasies to you, do not assume that they are losing their minds and do not attempt to force them into facing the truth. Listen quietly and, in time, as they begin to accept the reality of their child's death, these fantasies will disappear completely.

HELP WITH THE MOST DIFFICULT TASK

The most difficult task facing the parents is disposing of their child's clothing and treasured belongings. Handling these items evokes mental pictures of what once was, and intensifies their yearning for the past to be the present. Like the burial, it slams home the cruel reality of their child's death. Many parents have a hard time forcing themselves to get started. It is not uncommon or unusual for them to delay for a year or more. "Don't push the parents to clean out the dead child's things before they are ready," advises Deena. "But when it is time, offer to help and understand that there will be lots of tears."

The parents might choose to pack up everything in one fell swoop or they might want to do it a bit at a time. However they decide to do it, remember that they are emotionally debilitated and that they might make rash decisions they will later regret. "I have very few things of my son's and wish that I had kept more," continues Deena. "If the parents are unsure, don't throw anything out. It's not hurting anything, and having the personal belongings might actually help the parents in their grief."

When the parents are ready to clear out their child's room, you can provide sturdy boxes and tape and help them pack the boxes. If they are not ready to dispose of the belongings, you can offer to help store the boxes in a safe place. You can also offer to donate and to deliver any belongings the parents are sure they do want to dispose of to a suitable charity. Prior to making this offer, compile a list of organizations such as homeless shelters or centers for abused spouses and their children, and then allow the parents to select the organization. If you feel it appropriate you can also invite one or both of the parents to accompany you. It might be beneficial if they see firsthand that their child's belongings are going to help someone in need.

After the belongings are stored or disposed of, do not suggest that the parents immediately redecorate their child's room, or turn it into a guest room or study. But if they tell you that is their intention, offer to assist them in any way you can. Keep in mind that the parents are grieving deeply, and that they are exhausted both physically and mentally. They might be grateful if you offer to accompany them on shopping trips to the paint store and the fabric shop, or to help with the actual painting and redecorating.

DO NOT ADD TO THEIR GRIEF BY TEMPORARILY AVOIDING THEM OR BY PERMANENTLY DISAPPEARING FROM THEIR LIVES

When a child has been murdered, the parents feel as though they have been jettisoned from the mainstream of humanity. Their roles as mother and father are different. Their lives are different. In order to survive, they need to fit back in. They need to be included in everyday life. When others avoid them, they feel shunned and alone. "I have witnessed homicide survivors losing friends, spouses, children, and other close people who turn their backs after a murder occurs," explains Elsie. Losing the companionship of family members and close friends and being avoided by acquaintances cause the parents great pain. So why do some of us tend to do it?

It could very well be that we are genuinely afraid of saying or doing something that will sharpen their pain. Our stomachs churn as we ask ourselves: What should I say if they begin talking about the murder?

How should I respond if they begin to cry? Unfortunately, these troubling questions cannot be answered with a blanket statement. Each of us is a unique individual and we must handle encountering the parents in our own unique way. At the time of the encounter, you must decide how you will act and what you will say. To help you make this difficult decision, Deena advises, "If the situation is uncomfortable for you, try and imagine how the parents feel." When you see the parents you will respond appropriately if you remain calm and take a minute to remember Deena's advice.

If you suddenly and completely disappear from the parents' lives they are damaged in two ways. They feel abandoned. And they anguish over whether they have offended or upset you in some way.

When a friend of Jenny's dropped out of her life shortly after her daughter was murdered, Jenny suffered another loss and another form of grief. She explains, "In the months prior to my daughter's murder I had lent my support to a close friend when she suffered three losses quite close together—her mother, her sister, and her stepson. She and her husband came to our house the day after my daughter died, and they attended the funeral. Then she disappeared from my life. She did not return my calls, and I even wrote to her to see if somehow I had offended her. Two years later I called this friend again. She said she hadn't stayed in touch because she just didn't know what to say."

Not knowing what to say is probably the most common reason given for not seeing or communicating with the parents. On one hand, considering that it is a problem with which all of us grapple when anyone dies, it is a valid one. On the other hand, we know that relationships are based on trust. Even though the parents seem to be unable to concentrate on anything but their child's murder and their grief, you need to trust that, in the back of their minds, they are aware that words will sometimes fail you, just as words will sometimes fail them. After my daughter was murdered I knew that most of the people around me did not know what to say to me, and that I did not know what to say to them either. So I decided to tell them just that. To my surprise, I found that being open and honest with them helped ease the tension of the situation. And that, I believe, is why they continue to be supportive and understanding of my grief to this day.

Do not disappear from the parents' lives because you fear that your family will remind them that their's has become a permanently broken circle. If the parents are cut off from the day-to-day lives of other families, they are left with nothing but their grief. As they become more and more isolated, the familiar world they knew before they began to grieve begins to fade away. They can forget that one of the reasons they are battling their grief is to regain that world. The presence of you and your family in their lives will remind them of this.

Jenny's story continues. "The kicker was when this close friend said she was really glad that I had called because she and her daughter were having problems in their relationship, and she really needed someone to talk to!"

You might ask how a fellow parent could be so insensitive to the needs of a grieving parent. Our children are the most important people in our lives. When we are worried about them, as was Jenny's friend, our thoughts center around the cause of our worry and we tend not to think about anything or anyone else, even the feelings of a parent whose child has been murdered.

ALLOW THEM TO TALK ABOUT THEIR CHILD

For many years after the murder, any mention of their child might cause the parents to cry. This can mistakenly give family members, friends, and others the impression that talking about their child increases their pain. But the truth is this: They are in agony every minute of every day and sometimes this agony erupts in tears regardless of what is happening at that moment.

Crying when we are in pain is natural and normal. The bereaved parents' tears can be compared to the antiseptic a physician pours into a wound to clean out bacteria prior to treatment. Allowing the parents to talk and to cry freely is therapeutic. Eventually their tears will help wash away some of their torment and anguish. After Sandra's daughter was shot in the face by the daughter's boyfriend, Sandra found that the people who helped her the most were the friends who came by her house and let her talk. "But," she says, "only a few were brave enough to come by."

Since 1992, the year her daughter was shot in the back of the head, Jenny has also been fortunate to have a few brave friends. "My three best friends allow me to talk about my daughter any time I want to," she says. "Even though by now, they have heard the same story many times."

The company of others is also very beneficial to the grieving parents. After Patricia's daughter was stabbed to death, her daughter's daughter came to live with her. "Having my granddaughter living with me has helped," comments Patricia. "We talk about my daughter. We have cried together many times."

"Don't be afraid to discuss the child," adds Deena. "If you are unsure of how to approach the subject you could say, 'I don't want to hurt you but I want to talk about your son (or daughter).' If the parents don't want to talk about their child they will let you know."

You might find that the father is less likely to want to discuss the child than is the mother. This might stem from the fact that, for the most part, society deems it acceptable for women to cry but not men. If you are a male you can help by assuring the father than it is okay for him to cry; that you too would cry if your daughter or son, or another child who is important to you, died.

When the parents realize that family members and friends are not *turned off* by their tears, they might be more willing to talk about their child. As their pain begins to ease, sharing happy or amusing memories with others will help them immensely. The first time they laugh rather than cry when remembering their child—and this can take years—will make them aware that they are moving forward in the grieving process. It will give them hope for the future and the strength to carry on.

DON'T PUT LIMITS ON THEIR GRIEF

Interacting with the grieving parents and seeing them in severe pain is going to be traumatic no matter what type of relationship you share with them. Because you truly want them to be happy again, you might think it wise to advise them to put their child's murder and their grief behind them. But this is not wise.

When a female acquaintance gave Deena this advice, Deena was hurt and angry. "I almost slapped her," she explains. "Instead I told her off. And don't ever say to the parents, 'It's been X number of weeks, months, or years. Don't you think you should get over it and get on with life?' "

In our society we are much more accepting of persons with physical disabilities than we are with those suffering from grief. If a family member or friend has recurring cancer, we patiently offer them ongoing emotional support because we can see the physical effects of their disease. We know that they are locked in a life-and-death struggle. They are fighting to regain their health and to return to their normal lives.

The parents of a murdered child are also locked in a life-and-death struggle. They, like the cancer victim, are desperately fighting to save their lives. When you are having a difficult time interacting with them remind yourself that they did not choose for their child to be murdered. They did not choose to be in grief. And, unfortunately, they cannot choose the time when they will begin to assimilate the murder into their lives. When you remember these facts, you will realize why the parents' suffering worsens when they are urged to put their grief behind them. Instead of advising the parents to forget the brutal act that cruelly changed their lives, take a minute to consider what your life would be like if your daughter or son, or some other child who is important to you, was murdered. When you do, you will see that verbally acknowledging the negative changes that have taken place in the parents' lives and the turmoil these changes have caused is the best way to help them.

Many people, because they have not experienced murdered-child grief, have a tendency to compare it to other, more prevalent forms of grief such as divorce or the death of a mother or father. Comparing a known grief to an unknown one can give these people some insight into the pain the parents are feeling. But it can also cause them to develop an unrealistic expectation of when the parents should emerge from grief. "About six months after my daughter was shot to death," comments Pam, "a co-worker said to me, 'It only takes about six months to get over a divorce so you should be ready to put your daughter's death behind you and move on.' "

A similar statement was made to Joan approximately nine months after her son was shot in the back. "A friend who I talked to quite a bit," she says, "said to me, 'Don't you think it's time to let this go?' "

Statements such as these are extremely detrimental to the parents. They can subtly infer that they are not working hard enough to conquer their grief. They add to the heavy burden the parents are already carrying by causing them to question if they are abnormal because they are unable to free themselves from pain. In addition to fighting their grief, they now must fight unrealistic time limits set down by persons who have never walked in their shoes, and the parents can feel pressured to produce reasons why they are still in pain. When they run out of reasons, they can begin bottling their grief up inside and trying to pretend that it does not exist. If they are prevented from voicing their grief, it will fester and grow like a malignant tumor.

Patricia's daughter was stalked and stabbed to death only five years ago. "Yet," she says, "one person who calls himself my friend tells me I should not be grieving any more. To get over it!" Because the parents will always miss their child, they will always feel some amount of grief and pain. Telling them that they should not still be grieving at any point in time can be perceived by them to mean that their child's absence from their lives is not important to you. To have them perceive this statement in this way is not, of course, your intention. But, because the grieving parents are an exhausted bundle of raw nerve endings, they are extremely sensitive to all comments made to them, and they do not have the energy to dissect those comments to determine their true meaning.

Other types of statements can also infer that the child's absence from the parents' lives is not important. "When my son died I was pregnant with my daughter," explains Deena. "One day the manager of the store where I worked patted my rather large belly and said, 'I know that what you went through was tough but you have another on the way to take his place.' " Most members of our society can and do quickly replace a damaged or lost possession. If our car is destroyed in an accident, we buy another one. If our house burns down, we rebuild it. If our dog dies, we adopt a puppy. This mind set of modern day life can fool us into believing that nurturing a new baby, or their living children, will fill the void left in the parents' lives by the murder. Deena responds to this way of thinking by asking, "Now how in the world could my daughter ever take my son's place?"

There is no formula that dictates the length of time a person should grieve. In all probability, the parents of a murdered child will never fully recover. A full recovery is virtually impossible because they will never be able to forget the brutality and savagery of their child's death.

DO NOT BE JUDGMENTAL

Because every parent grieves differently, and because there is no right or wrong way to grieve, the grief behaviors of one parent cannot be compared to those of another. Some will visit their child's grave daily. Others will visit only on holidays. Some will engage in frantic, and often useless, activity. Others will withdraw and become inactive. Some will want to be with other people almost every minute of every day. Others will need to be alone for hours at a time. Some will cry frequently. Others will hardly ever cry.

Because one parent behaves one way and the other the opposite, does not mean that one is grieving more deeply than the other. You must be careful not to judge the depth of the parents' grief by how they behave when you are with them. "When my son died, I went out into public every day because I had to," says Deena. "I had to appear in court. I had to go to work. When going out into public I neither cried nor did I act hysterical. All strong emotions were saved for private. It's too difficult to explain to people the reason for your bizarre actions, and no parent should have to explain."

Regardless of how often you communicate with the parents, and how much they share with you, you cannot know what actually motivates them to behave in a certain way at a certain time. You can help by not comparing them to other bereaved persons you have known—either in your own mind or while you are talking with other people. When the parents realize that you accept their grief behaviors, no matter how different they are from the grief behaviors of other bereaved individuals, they will feel more comfortable being with you. And they will be more receptive to the ways in which you are trying to assist them.

Despite this there will be times when the parents reject your assistance and your suggestions as to how they can help themselves. Most often these suggestions stem from your personal experiences and preferences. If, in the past, you suffered the death of a loved one, or some other type of loss, you found that certain behaviors and activities helped you work through your grief. For instance, you might have drawn closer to your family, volunteered to work at a hospice, or attended church more frequently. When you suggest one of these activities to the grieving parents they might heed your suggestion. But do not be hurt or offended if it does not help them in the same way it helped you. Filiberto explains, "My wife and I tried, and even became members of a church," he says. "But that hurt even more. We stopped attending because we were not ready for it. We have bad feelings about sermons referring to guardian angels over children, and about God."

If the first activity you suggest to the parents does not work out be prepared to suggest a second, a third, and a fourth. If you offer to participate in the activity with them, it will be easier for them to accept your suggestion.

DO NOT FORGET THEIR CHILD

One of the parents' worst fears is that other people will eventually forget their child. They will remember their child for the remainder of their lives and they hope that everyone they know will do the same.

Over time you can alleviate the parents' fear by continuing to verbally share your memories of their child with them, visiting the cemetery, or incorporating a small memento into holiday celebrations, weddings, graduations, and other special occasions. Jenny's friends send cards on her daughter's birthday and on her death date. "They do this," comments Jenny, "to let me know that they are thinking about her."

For several years prior to her death, Sandra's daughter worked as a nanny. "She was loved by so many but especially by children," says Sandra. "So many sent cards telling me something special she had done for their child. They often sent a picture of her with that child. Some children even wrote me letters."

Sharing your memories of the child in a letter to the parents is very beneficial. As the years go by they will reread your letter and be pleased that you thought their child was special in some unique way.

Sending the parents a "thinking about you" card on holidays, on their birthdays, and on Mother's Day and Father's Day is also a good idea. When choosing a card that is appropriate, keep in mind that these days will be difficult for them for many years after the murder. Their birthdays will not be happy and their Christmases will not be merry because they miss their child.

Do not think that reminding the parents of their child is going to enhance their pain. Whenever you encounter them in the grocery store, the mall, or the library, you will naturally ask about their living children. It is just as natural for you to mention the child that was murdered by, perhaps, recounting a memory you have of the child. The parents will be grateful that you have not forgotten.

ALLOW THEM TO VENT THEIR RAGE

The word rage terrifies all of us because we associate it with devastating destruction. We describe a rain-swollen river that is overflowing its banks and sweeping away everything in its path as "raging." We say that the damaging winds produced by a hurricane "rage" rather than "blow."

In most cases the parents are enraged by what has happened to their child, to them, and to their lives. They are acutely aware that they need to keep their rage under control. They often do everything in their power to keep it hidden from the outside world because, explains Jenny, "The enormity of this emotion can often scare the people witnessing it."

Being forced to hide their rage only increases it. If the grieving parents are not allowed to vent their rage in positive ways, it can destroy their lives and the lives of those around them. There are many theories as to how humans can safely vent rage. Some say it can be worked off by punching a pillow or a punching bag, screaming aloud in a closed room, or exercising vigorously. Others state that rage can be dissipated by writing a letter to the person with whom we are enraged or by describing it in a daily journal.

In most cases, these methods will be of little, if any, help to the parents of a murdered child. Their rage, like their grief, lasts for many years and is extremely complex. It is not directed toward a single person or event; it reaches out in many directions. It can, for example, be directed toward the person who savaged their child, or toward the killer's parents for having reared a person capable of committing a cold-blooded murder. It can be directed toward society for producing violent movies and television shows written to entertain rather than raise awareness of the devastation a murder causes, or toward the criminal justice system that seems to be more interested in protecting the rights of the murderer than in meting out punishment equal to the crime committed. It can even be directed toward their child for leaving them, at God for taking their child, or at themselves for allowing the murder to happen.

You can help the parents by giving them opportunities to verbally express their rage. When they do—and this will happen time and time again—soothe them by acknowledging that they have every right to be enraged, or by listening quietly until the storm passes. Allowing the parents to vent their rage in your presence is not going to be easy for you. You might find that witnessing their display of this powerful emotion is embarrassing and/or frightening. If possible try not to show what you are feeling. Do not abruptly change the subject or flee the room in a panic. Instead, wait and see what the parents are going to do next and then follow their lead. Venting their rage might thoroughly exhaust them, and they might want to be alone to rest and regroup. Or, in their ongoing effort to manage their grief by keeping in touch with the world around them, they might be the ones who abruptly change the subject. Be prepared to quickly enter into a conversation about the current price of a dozen eggs, or some other trivial subject. At the same time, keep in mind that some parents require physical as well as emotional support. If this is the case, when the storm of their rage is over, wipe away their tears or give them a gentle hug, but only if you truly feel comfortable doing so.

Verbal expression might also come in the form of plotting revenge. "Don't think the parents are grim or completely out of it if they talk about vengeance," says Deena. "Chances are that they never got enough justice and they need these fantasies to help them through." It will be extremely difficult for you to listen to the parents plot revenge. You will worry and ask yourself if they are capable of carrying through on their desire to avenge their child's murder. More than likely they are not. "But," continues Deena, "if they start to hire someone to kill the murderer, step in and stop them."

You will also need to step in if the parents begin to vent their rage on other people by provoking arguments or fist fights, or if they begin to participate in life-threatening activities. This does not mean that you are going to try and prevent them from taking up boxing or skydiving. But if they begin to seek out confrontations with others, to drink heavily, or to depend on drugs to get them through the day, you can encourage them to talk through their rage with you. If this does not work, you can suggest that they become members of a support group for parents of murdered children. Your local library can provide information on groups that the parents can join. If your community does not have such a group, you can contact an existing group in another county or state for advice on how to establish one. And, even though it was not your child who was murdered, you can offer to help the parents organize the group.

For those parents who are participating in life-threatening activities, but who are not interested in becoming members of an existing support group or in establishing a new one, you can suggest that they see a mental health professional. Before making this suggestion, however, research the professionals practicing in the parents' community. Not all therapists are familiar with the complexities and extended trauma of murdered-child grief and, if the parents see such a therapist, they can be seriously harmed. After Evelyn's nineteen-year-old daughter was stabbed to death, she sought to resolve her unbearable grief by going to a psychiatrist. "But all he did," she explains, "was tell me to exercise and get busy."

This advice might be appropriate for some types of grief, but it is inappropriate for murdered-child grief. These parents require an environment where they can freely vent and work through their feelings. Although exercising frequently and keeping busy can help them survive the trauma of their child's murder it will do little to help them assimilate it into their lives. I know this from personal experience. Even though my daughter was shot to death in 1983, there are still times I need to talk about her murder. As incomprehensible as it might seem, there are still times I cannot believe that I and my family are the victims of such a senseless act of violence.

* * *

Ninety-nine percent of the time the parents of a murdered child regain their lives with the help of their families, friends, co-workers, homicide or bereavement support groups, and their own courage and determination. The help you give during the initial phases of their grief will enable them to eventually help themselves. When they do begin to help themselves, you and they will be happy that you took the time to offer your support and understanding. And you will realize why it is necessary for you to continue being supportive by encouraging the parents to seek out activities that will someday help them lead lives that are productive, and somewhat happy and free from pain.

CHAPTER 8

Immediate Ways the Parents of a Murdered Child Help Themselves

> My awareness that there are so many, many people that are hurting because of crime is one reason I was motivated to survive.
>
> *Chet*
> *1-23-96*

> We owe it to ourselves to be the best we can despite our loss, but it will never be easy. We will get used to the pain the same way we would get used to the loss of an arm or leg. It is gone, and we have no choice. But we still miss that part.
>
> *Beckie*
> *11-22-95*

Over the course of a lifetime all of us will experience one or more losses. These losses can begin in childhood with the death of a beloved pet, teacher, or grandparent. In adulthood most of us will suffer the deaths of our parents, a spouse or lover, or a close friend. Our responses to these significant losses will depend on the roles the deceased played in our lives. The period of pain and suffering that accompanies each loss will differ in intensity and duration. Because we are unique individuals, and because there is no right or wrong way to grieve, the methods each of us use to work through our grief will also be different.

I use the term *work through our grief* rather than the word *recover* because there are some types of loss from which it is impossible to fully recover. To understand these types of loss, pretend for a moment that you have a sister and a brother. Your sister is suffering with a bad cold. Your brother is suffering with sore shoulder muscles torn in an accident. In a week or so, when you ask your sister how she is feeling, she will respond that she is fine. The cold is completely gone. When you ask your brother the same question he will respond that his torn muscles have healed. However, he adds, due to scar tissue that formed at the site of each tear during the healing process, his doctor has informed him that he will, at times, feel pain in his shoulder for the remainder of his life.

The emotional injuries sustained by parents when their child is murdered will, like your brother's torn muscles, eventually heal. But the scar tissue that forms during both healing processes leaves behind its own type of permanent damage that causes its own type of permanent pain. And so the persons who suffered these injuries will say that, although their injuries have healed, they will never make a full recovery. Their emotional or physical condition will never again be as good as it was prior to receiving the injuries, and they must learn to live their lives accordingly.

Jenny, whose only child, a daughter, died in 1992 after being shot in the back of the head, does not use the word *recover* when talking about her grief. "I believe," she says, "that this word is inappropriate with regards to the journey from being a *victim* to being a *survivor.* A better word would be *reconstruct.* We learn coping tools in our reconstruction. Although we still have bad days—birth dates and death dates will always be difficult—we learn to laugh again, to smile, to cherish each day and the people around us. But we cannot *recover* because to *recover* would mean we are not changed by the experience. It would mean that our child's murder made no difference in our life."

After carrying the burden of the murders of two of his four sons for more than five years, a burden so oppressive that most of us, not even other bereaved parents, can begin to imagine its crushing weight, Chet also believes that the parents of murdered children do not recover. "We cope," he states. "We survive. We try to get through each day. We try to stay sane through tomorrow. I think we all experience the awfulness of constantly enduring that screeching light that keeps going off in our heads. That shouts, 'My child is dead.' But then we remember the next horrible line, 'Because somebody killed him.' And there is no closure, no acceptance. The pain never ends."

When interacting with the parents of a murdered child, it is important for you to remember that they know, deep in their hearts, they are not going to make a full recovery. Telling them that they will—especially by using trite, hackneyed expressions such as, "time heals all wounds"—frustrates the parents. They do not ask that you understand their grief, but they do expect you to accept it as the lifelong trauma it is. Larry, who in 1994, began living with the harsh reality that his son was shot to death execution-style, explains, "I might learn to live with the heartache, the hate, the emptiness, and the wanting to see and be with him," he says, "but I don't think I will ever recover from this."

The parents also ask that you see the murder of their child for what it truly is—a loss which shatters their lives so completely that, no matter how hard they try, they cannot piece the fragments back together. When you refuse to see the reality of their shattered lives, you prove to them that you are not listening to what they are attempting to tell you about their grief. You push them away from you and from other people who might be able to help them.

It is also important to remember that when the parents learned of the murder, their status in life changed. Rather than being anonymous faces in the sea of faces populating our world, they now stand out as being the parents of a murdered child. From being an average family, living in an average house on an average street in an average neighborhood, they become grist for the media mill. Their pain-wracked faces are seen on the morning news. The gory details of the murder are printed in the evening newspaper. Their grief, as well as their lives and the life of their child, are spread out for review and discussed by everyone in their community. If the murder is extremely gruesome, it can even receive statewide or national attention.

When the parents are thrust into the glare of the public eye, they feel like unrehearsed actors who are suddenly thrust on stage under the glare of a spotlight. Unprepared and vulnerable, the parents, like the actors, feel lost and alone. Despite their feelings of aloneness and vulnerability, most parents brave the curiosity of the public and the media to attend the murderer's trial. Sandra, whose daughter died after being shot in the face by the daughter's boyfriend, states that attending his trial was extremely painful. "But," she explains, "it was also one of the things that helped me the most. I could support my daughter's memory when I couldn't be there to hold her as she gasped for breath and died."

Sandra's reason for attending the trial points out two of the horrors that continue to haunt the parents. They could not protect their child from being savaged by a brutal person, and they could not be there to comfort their child at the moment of death. Somehow the parents must learn to live with these horrors. And, with ongoing support from the people who love them, they somehow do.

"I was also helped," continues Sandra, "when I was allowed to voice my feelings at the sentencing hearing." The opportunity to give the court what is commonly referred to as a Victim Impact Statement is another reason most parents feel compelled to attend the trial. Giving such a statement allows them to talk publicly about their child—a privilege they might never have again. It is also the only chance they might have to describe the devastating affect the murder has had on their lives. Because of this devastating affect, the parents want to do everything in their power to ensure that the killer will not go unpunished. And, even though what they see and hear in the courtroom is excruciatingly painful and traumatic, they need to witness him or her being tried, and hopefully, convicted.

When the trial is over, and the parents are no longer in the public eye, they undertake the task of rebuilding their lives. At this point they, like Jenny, begin thinking of themselves as both victims and survivors. This dual role into which they were thrust so abruptly, changed the way they approach the business of living. Although they no longer take life for granted, they must continually struggle to survive.

How and why they manage to survive are as singular as the parents themselves; each must accomplish it in his or her own way. Survival, as they soon discover, is a multifaceted process that evolves over time.

In order to survive, the parents must first make a solemn vow to continue to live. The necessity of making this vow might seem strange to those who have not experienced murdered-child grief, but it must be done. After my daughter was shot in the head, I was in such pain I contemplated suicide. Physically and emotionally I was hurting so badly death would have been a pleasant relief. But I knew I could not die. My husband, my living children, my mother, and sisters still needed me. So I made a conscious decision to live.

Making the decision to live, because it condemns the parents to a lifetime of some degree of pain and suffering, is a true test of their courage. Although they might not discuss their decision with you, or even be aware that they have made it, you can provide positive reinforcement by acknowledging their ongoing pain and commenting affirmatively on their willingness to move forward in life in spite of it.

While not all parents desire to end their lives, most of them would like nothing more than to withdraw from the world. Dealing with the multiple traumas of their grief, and of the murder and the varied reactions of others to it, causes exhaustion. When coupled with the stresses and problems of everyday life, the parents fear that they are going to be totally overwhelmed. In the dark of the night, when sleep eludes them, they ask if they have the strength to handle it all. Then, because they have determined that they are survivors as well as victims, they tell themselves they do have the strength.

After Beckie's son was shot to death on a public street while walking his girlfriend home from work, Beckie decided that the killers had already taken enough from her and her family. "I could not, would not, let them have more," she states emphatically.

At the time of her son's murder, Beckie was operating a day-care center in her home. After the murder, working with young children must have painfully reminded her of the time when her son was a young child. To save herself from this added pain, it would have been easy for her to close the center. But, because she stood firm in her resolve not to let the killers take anything else away from her, she kept it open.

Beckie's refusal to withdraw from the life she had been living before the murder, or even to back away from it temporarily, rewarded her in a surprising and beneficial way. "I found," she says, "that the toddlers and babies kept me sane and balanced with their innocence and love."

For the majority of parents, refusing to allow their lives to be completely destroyed by the murder is not sufficient to ensure their survival. They know they need to do more. Doing more sometimes means learning as much as they can about their bereavement. Evelyn's nineteen-year-old daughter was stabbed to death in 1984. "After her death," explains Evelyn, "I read everything on grieving parents I could get my hands on. That helped me so much."

Other parents gain an understanding of their bereavement by writing about it. In order to write down what they are feeling they must probe and analyze their emotions. Although this is an extremely painful process they find that taking the time to physically transfer their thoughts and feelings onto paper can be therapeutic.

In 1989, shortly after Margie's twenty-seven-year-old daughter was brutally stabbed twenty-four times by the daughter's husband, Margie decided that keeping a journal would aid her in understanding the many grief emotions churning inside her. "I write in my journal just about every day," she says. "It helps me to reach some of my inner feelings. Even if it makes me cry when I write something, that is okay. It is a good release."

"Writing has been an integral part of my healing therapy too," adds Beckie. "At first I kept a journal. Then I wrote for our support group's newsletter, and eventually other avenues opened up for my writing."

When Lois' son was shot to death in 1975 by an escaped convict hiding out in one of the houses her son was building, Lois began keeping a diary. "I kept my diary from the first moment for about eight years," she says.

To those of you who have not experienced the murder of your child, Margie's seven years and Lois' eight years might seem like an excessively long time to analyze murdered-child grief. But it is not. The emotions of grief are buried, layer upon layer, deep inside the parents.

Uncovering each layer is a laborious task that can be compared to the task undertaken by an archeologist who digs, carefully and methodically, to uncover fragile artifacts. If you learn that one or both of the parents with whom you are interacting have been keeping a diary or a journal for several years, you might mistakenly begin to believe that the analysis they are doing has become an obsession with their grief rather than a form of self-designed therapy. If you are tempted to think this way, you need to remember that, when faced with a lifetime of missing their child, seven or eight years is not a long time to the parents.

In addition to learning all they can about their grief, the parents must also learn to cope with it. One of the most common coping mechanisms is creating ways to include their murdered child in their everyday lives. Including their child is neither morbid nor abnormal. The parents think about their child every day and often express their thoughts in tangible ways. For the past seven years, Margie and Kenneth have had to live with the knowledge that their son-in-law murdered their daughter. Coping with this excruciatingly painful fact has been extremely difficult. One of the ways they manage to cope is by making weekly visits to the cemetery where their daughter's ashes are buried. "We have beautiful plants there in the summer," comments Margie. "We decorate these plants differently for each holiday. When winter comes our florist makes a planter of spruce tips upon which we put little angels. This gives us a feeling of our daughter being part of a special day, at least spiritually."

Joan, whose thirty-eight-year-old son was shot in the back at close range with a shotgun, also finds that visiting the cemetery helps her to cope with her grief. "I go to the cemetery quite a bit," she says, "and I change the flowers for the different holidays. This isn't a custom in my family, but I feel the need to do it even if I believe that isn't really where my son's spirit is."

All of us share special relationships with a variety of people. And each of these relationships contain moments of note and traditions known only to those sharing the relationship. Sandra, in the four years since her daughter was murdered, has frequently visited the grave. "I put little things on her grave that were special between her and I," she states, "like ravioli." It is not unusual for Joan, or other grieving parents, to place what some might consider to be non-traditional remembrances on their child's grave. If you are very close to the parents, and want to let them know that talking about their child will not make you uncomfortable, gently and tactfully ask them about any objects you see on the grave. The act of inquiring, when handled properly, can make it easier for them to talk with you about their child, now and in the future.

For many grieving parents, ensuring that their child's life is remembered by family members and friends is also necessary for their survival. "I talk about my daughter a lot," comments Margie. "I want people to know that it's okay to talk about her. I want them to so she won't be forgotten."

Some parents also want their child to be remembered in ways that are more concrete. Mary's son, prior to being sexually assaulted and beaten to death, was working toward a career in the creative arts. As a permanent tribute to his talents and interests in life, and to help increase awareness of the need for victim's rights, Mary and her husband Robert designed and produced one square of a quilt that is publicly displayed in their home state during Victim's Rights Week. "My husband and I worked on it together with almost a perverse sort of determination and dedication," she states, "so that people can awaken to the realization that they too can be victims of murder and violence."

Like Mary's son, all children harbor dreams of future accomplishments and glories. Because their child was robbed of those dreams when he or she was robbed of life, the parents can yearn to bring at least one of them to fruition. Before she was strangled, Filiberto's fourteen-year-old daughter was engaged in many activities including writing poetry. "After she died," says Filiberto, "my wife submitted poems our daughter had written to a national poetry organization. One was selected and published in a book of poems. My wife is doing her best to make our daughter's dream come true—to be famous."

The parents' desire to ensure that their child and their child's life will not be forgotten is easily understood by all people. What is harder for many people to understand is some parents' desire to ensure that their child's death will be remembered as well. These people think that, because the murder was so horrible, the parents should want to forget the details rather than remember them. But what they fail to understand is that, because the death of their child cruelly and permanently changed their lives, it is impossible for the parents to forget. Rather than waste precious energy struggling to forget what they truly cannot, they need to assimilate the murder into their lives so that they can accept its reality and devote their full energies to reconstructing their lives. Joan chose to preserve the memory of her son's death in a very creative way. "I made a scrapbook of all the cards we got," she says, "and newspaper clippings, legal papers, etc."

Some mental health professionals espouse the theory that, in order to heal from grief, bereaved persons must accept the death of their loved one as a natural part of life. Although it is true that all living creatures eventually die, this is not an appropriate theory to present to grieving parents—especially the parents of a murdered child. Keeping a scrapbook of mementos from their child's death is, for some parents, no different from keeping a scrapbook of mementos from their child's life. It might even point out the fact that they have accepted the death. Accepting the death, however, is not the same as being at peace with their loss. I have finally reconciled myself to the fact that my daughter is dead, and I have learned to live with it. But I will never stop missing her. And I will never think that, because she once lived, it is natural for her to be dead.

Joan, in addition to filling a scrapbook with mementos of her son's murder, knew that she had to do more if she was going to reconstruct her life. When her son was shot in the back, he was taken to a trauma center where he lived for eighteen days. "After he died," she says, "I made myself get out, call friends, get involved outside myself."

Many parents opt to survive by forcing themselves to become involved in new activities. In 1976, after her daughter was raped, beaten, and run over by a car, Christina began a program of physical exercise that continues today. "I work out two hours each day," she states. "This keeps me from getting depressed. When it gets really bad, I put on my earphones and go for a walk."

Although every day can be depressing, for many parents the most depressing are the dates of their child's birth, death, and burial. Every year on these dates, they might need to spend the long, sad hours doing something they have never done before. Jenny's daughter was buried the day before Thanksgiving. "With the anniversary of the crime, my daughter's death date, and burial date always at Thanksgiving," she says, "it has become the least favorite and most dreaded holiday of the year. We go to Mexico to deal with these difficult days. We can cry, be in a bad mood, and not have to justify our behavior to those who just want to be merry and give thanks."

Dreading the merriment of holidays is but one more aspect of murdered-child grief with which the parents must learn to cope. If, for a while, they refuse to celebrate, or choose to absent themselves from the festivities, family members and friends should not be offended or think that the parents are not handling their grief well. Instead they should realize that they are merely doing what they need to do to survive.

If, on the other hand, the parents choose to celebrate holidays from the very beginning of their grief, the people around them should not think that their suffering has already eased to a bearable level. The year our daughter died, my husband and I discussed what we would do on Christmas Day. We decided to observe the holiday as a way of celebrating our two living children (both adults) and our granddaughter. As we moved through the day we pretended to be enjoying ourselves when, in fact, we were suffering terribly. Other families with whom we celebrated were whole and happy. Ours was a broken circle. One of our children was missing.

After surviving the merriment of Christmas, we were faced with the prospect of surviving the merriment of New Year's Eve. Before our daughter's death we had always welcomed in the new year by attending a party or by going out to a nightclub. What would we do this year? Our twenty-one-year-old son saw our dilemma and suggested that, rather than going out, we invite our parents and some of their friends, all widows and widowers who knew what it was like to experience grief, to our house to play cards. We acted on his suggestion, and again, despite our misery, managed to survive.

By staying home that year we established a new family tradition. On New Year's Eve we now gather together in one of our homes to celebrate. The card games, however, have been replaced with rollicking games of Charades. The elderly folks keep score and cheer on those attempting to act out the titles of books, movies, and songs. The children who are too young to participate, watch in amazement as their parents, aunts, uncles, and older siblings quack like ducks, wiggle like snakes, or do whatever else comes to mind that will enable their team to guess the title they are acting out. Everyone has a good time, and we find that the physical activity helps us work through the grief pain we still feel.

Avoiding holiday celebrations, or abruptly abandoning old traditions and establishing new ones, can lead some people to mistakenly believe that the parents are not handling their grief well. Unfortunately, there are also other behaviors or activities that can be misconstrued as an inability to handle their grief, or, even worse, as refusal by the parents to let go of their child and to accept the death. Sandra's daughter was murdered in 1993. "But," she says, "I sometimes hold her picture, and hug it, and cry until I feel like I've been able to be close to her." Although it is possible for the parents to accept the death, it is impossible for them to let go of the child their bodies created. No human is expected to let go of happy memories created by past experiences, and grieving parents should not be expected to let go of happy memories of their child. These memories are precious to them, and they should be encouraged to nurture them. "I have memories of my daughter that not even her killer can take away from me," states Margie. Keeping their child's memory alive, by holding a picture, or by listening to their child's voice on a tape recording, or rereading a poem written by their child, is not an indication that the parents are not handling their grief well. Instead, it is an indication that they are helping themselves to survive. And it should be acknowledged as such.

Once the parents have begun to help themselves by taking better care of their physical and mental health, they often turn to improving or safe-guarding their emotional health by reaching out to others in need. Reaching out helps the parents in several ways. It channels the negativity of their grief into positive activities. Because they must concentrate on someone else's pain, reaching out to others temporarily takes their minds off of their own pain. And, in an oblique way, it allows them to continue the caregiver role they assumed when they became parents. Christina reaches out to others in need on a regular basis. "I do volunteer work at a hospice," she states, "and I work with abused children." Although Christina did not begin doing volunteer work to gain recognition, so many people have benefitted from her work, the residents of her hometown have honored her with several awards including the Woman of Character Award.

Carol, whose son was shot by the man her family had taken under its wing when the man was a child, also uses her pain to benefit other people. At the time of the murder Carol and her husband Jim were living out of state. Several hours after the murder, the tenant to whom they were leasing their house in their home state gave the local police Carol and Jim's new address. The local police then passed the new address on to the police in the state where Carol and Jim were residing, asking that they be notified of their son's death. "But," says Carol, "the police here did not follow through and never informed us. An elderly neighbor of our son finally located our current address and called to tell us that our son was dead. 'I'm positive he is dead,' she said. 'I seen his brains all over the furniture and the wall and the rug.' " The elderly woman's words, because they were so gruesomely graphic, were permanently burned into Carol's heart. To ensure that other parents of murdered children would not receive the news of their child's death in the same horrible manner, Carol began accompanying the police on all violent death notification calls.

Other parents choose to reach out to those in need in less structured ways. Pam's twenty-two-year-old daughter was shot to death during a robbery in the daughter's home. "After the court hearings and the sentencing were over, I started contacting other parents of murdered children as I saw them on television or read about them in the newspaper," she says. "I knew they probably felt all alone, like I had, and I wanted them to know that I would be there for them if and when they needed someone to talk to that could truly understand what they were going through."

Feeling alone, even when surrounded by people who care deeply, is another unsettling aspect of murdered-child grief. Despite the efforts of family members and friends (and even other bereaved parents whose children have died from causes other than murder) to listen and to understand, some parents of a murdered child gain comfort only by talking with other parents of murdered children. "I tried a support group for bereaved parents," explains Chet. "I still go occasionally. But I am a member of an elite group of bereaved parents. I don't fit in the general category."

Parents of a murdered child who prefer the company of other parents of murdered children are not insinuating that their pain is any greater than that of parents who have miscarried, given birth to a stillborn, or have lost a child due to an illness, an accident, or a birth defect. The death of a child is a devastating tragedy no matter how it happens. But, because someone deliberately chose to take their children's lives, in some cases a person they loved and trusted, the grief of parents whose children have been murdered definitely is different. Also, because murderers are seldom kept in prison—or executed—but come up for parole instead, the parents are forced to relive their nightmare every time a parole hearing is scheduled. If the wound left by their child's murder has begun to scab over, the criminal justice system sees to it that the scab is ripped off again, and again, and again.

"There is also dealing with the police, the detectives, and the attorneys," states Pam. "And worst of all, coming face to face with the last human being to see our child alive and who is also their killer."

Deena, whose two-year-old son was asphyxiated by Deena's ex-husband, has also reached out to others in need by contacting parents whose children have died. "When I learned of a mother whose child had died of SIDS," she says, "I put a personal note in a card and had that delivered with flowers. I told her of my experience and that she should call anytime she felt the need. I spent three hours on the phone with her one night talking and crying. We even laughed a couple of times. She told me that what I had done had helped her a lot."

Reaching out to others in need does not have to be done by personal contact. After Mary and Robert's son was murdered by a known criminal who was given probation rather than jail time, they agreed to be interviewed by a staff writer for *Reader's Digest*. "He did an article about criminals who are set free to commit another crime," explains Mary.

Patricia, whose twenty-six-year-old daughter was stalked and stabbed to death by a man whom the daughter alleged had attempted to sexually molest her child, has also spoken publicly about the murder and her grief. "Shortly after my daughter's death," she states, "I was on a half-hour talk show with the local Chief of Police. I have much more to say about all the injustices dealing with my daughter's case. I have written a summary to send to the television talk show."

Speaking with strangers about the circumstances surrounding their child's death is, for all parents, a painful and unsettling experience. Despite this, in the hope that they can prevent the murder of another child, spare another parent similar anguish, and make the general public aware of the flaws and inconsistencies in our criminal justice systems, they are willing to do it.

Many parents, in order to purge their pain, prefer to talk about the murder in familiar settings with people they know well. Sadly, some of them find that their family members and friends, and others with whom they come in contact, choose not to discuss the murder with them. "Murder is a distasteful thing," explains Mary, "and no one wants to face its reality or deal with it. Because few want to discuss murder, we paid a competent (mental health) professional."

After her son was murdered, Lois also sought the help of a mental health professional. "Dr. Elisabeth Kübler-Ross helped me first by letters and phone," says Lois. "Then I attended her one-week workshop."

Because I do not want to leave you with the erroneous impression that most grieving parents require formal counseling, it should be noted that Mary's eighteen-year-old son and Lois' twenty-four-year-old son were both murdered by convicted criminals. One had been given probation rather than jail time. The other had escaped from prison. Had the legislators in the states in which the murders were committed enacted stronger laws, or the criminal justice systems carried out their responsibilities more efficiently, both of these intelligent, productive young men might be alive today. Knowing that a child's life could have been spared, is a crushing burden no parent should ever be asked to carry. Perhaps without the counseling of mental health professionals, neither Mary nor Lois would have survived its weight.

While some parents rely on mental health professionals to help them survive their child's murder, others rely on their faith in God. Carolyn, whose son was an unarmed security guard who died after being shot four times during a robbery in the bus station where he was employed, explains, "I have been trying very hard to get as close to God as possible," she says, "and depend upon Him to lean on and get through this."

Joan also attributes her faith with helping her a great deal. "Without my faith, I don't think I could have survived this," she says.

Mental health professionals who have a thorough knowledge of murdered-child grief, and the parents' faith in a supreme being, are two sources of strength upon which the parents can draw. But, as explained by Sandra, there is another important source that should not be overlooked. "One of the strengths I have," she comments, "is a strong, stable marriage."

While it is true that many marriages fail after the murder, it is also true that other marriages grow stronger. Ten years after our daughter was murdered, my husband and I were on the brink of divorce. Although neither of us pointed the finger of blame at the other, as some couples do, our problem was that the way in which each of us was grieving was so different from the other, we had drifted apart. Then, when we realized a divorce would allow the murderer to completely destroy our lives, my husband and I began the difficult task of getting to know the new person each of us had become. We discussed the individual ways in which our grief manifested itself, and agreed to support, encourage, and accept those ways even if we did not understand them. Today, our marriage is a safe and secure haven from our grief.

* * *

As you can see, parents of murdered children begin reconstructing their lives by using a variety of creative techniques. It cannot be assumed that one technique is better than another. All parents should be encouraged to develop their own, and then act accordingly.

The parents who participated in my research for this book each found that learning to cope with their agony and rage was extremely difficult. The actual act of surviving was even more difficult.

They also found that learning to cope and managing to survive are multiphased processes. To successfully work through these processes, each parent employed a combination of short- and long-term techniques. Examples of short-term techniques were discussed in this chapter. Long-term techniques are discussed in the next chapter.

CHAPTER 9

Future Ways the Parents of a Murdered Child Help Themselves

My support group really helped me the most. Being around other parents that you know feel emotions like yours.

Patricia
2-13-96

Since it is a lifetime of adjustment without my son, I give help to others who have had a loss. I have regained a balance in my life with my son's death as a part of it.

Lois
12-22-95

In order for you to understand that the parents of a murdered child engage in a lifelong struggle to survive their child's murder, you need only recall Jenny's comment that she and her family were given life sentences when her daughter was murdered. In the beginning, most parents do not realize that they have been condemned to a lifetime of pain and suffering; they are too busy coping with the initial phases of their grief, the traumas of the police investigation, and, if an arrest has been made, the trial of the alleged murderer.

When the parents do realize their fate, they begin searching for long-term activities that will help them survive. Some become members of groups established to help bereaved persons deal with their grief. Some join forces with other survivors of violent crime in organizations working to turn the tide of violence that, they believe, threatens to destroy our world.

A sampling of these groups and organizations will be covered in this chapter. But before we delve into them, you need to know that events continually occur which threaten the parents' ability to survive. For example, when the teenage male who killed Jenny's daughter was released from prison after serving only twenty-seven months of a forty-one month sentence, he was ordered to pay restitution. "He is supposed to pay all costs associated with my daughter's burial," explains Jenny. To date this young killer has, for the most part, ignored the restitution order. "I have been back to court five times in the last year," Jenny continues. "Each time it is so hard for me to have to look at him." Only the parent of a murdered child can fully understand how traumatic these court appearances are for Jenny, and why they set her back in her effort to reconstruct her life.

Mary also suffered a set-back when she read in a 1995 magazine that a Northeastern state had approved a group seeking to legalize pedophilia as a legitimate non-profit organization. The approval allows this group, which explained it was established to conduct charitable, literary, scientific, and educational activities, to receive charitable donations, and taxpayer-financed grants. When Mary came across this announcement, she was incensed. Remembering the condition of her son's badly disfigured body after he was sexually assaulted and beaten to death by a man twice arrested for sexually assaulting young boys, she asked, "Where is society headed?"

Many parents of murdered children are asking the same question. Still suffering from the death of their child, they, like Mary, scan newspaper and magazine articles. Each parent looks for signs that their elected officials are leaning toward spending more of their tax dollars on victims' rights rather than giving them away to groups such as the one described above. Each parent looks for signs that their elected officials are writing new laws geared to deterring crime rather than defending old laws that have become ineffective. Each parent looks for signs that prosecuting attorneys are asking that convicted criminals be sentenced to prison rather than allowing them to plea bargain their way back into society. Each parent looks for signs that judges are beginning to punish criminals to the full extent of the law rather than giving them reduced sentences.

When these parents see that little of this is happening, many of them become activists. Propelled by their rage and fueled by their agony, they strive to make changes in our criminal justice systems that will establish rights for victims or widen the scope of existing rights.

Chet is one of the parents who became an activist. "After my sons died," he explains, "I felt helpless because honest, God-fearing, hard-working fathers and mothers of our community didn't realize the danger they and their children were in. I realized that I had some clout because of the horrors I had lived through. And I had an urgent need to do something that might prevent other parents from going through this hell."

To help overcome his feeling of helplessness, Chet joined a victim's assistance network in his home state. As chairperson of the legislative committee of this network, he devoted much time to meeting with the Governor, the Attorney General, the Director of the State Bureau of Investigation, the Prison Director, and members of the senate and house of delegates. In these meetings, Chet requested that an amendment be added to the state constitution that would guarantee crime victims the right to be informed of all criminal proceedings involving crimes committed against them or members of their families. The amendment would also guarantee victims the right to be present during these proceedings and to tell how the crime had adversely affected their lives.

During Chet's all-out war to have a victim's rights amendment added to his state's constitution, he voiced his agony and his outrage whenever and wherever he could. Because of this, he attracted the attention of several newspaper reporters who wrote comprehensive articles about him. As word of Chet's battle spread, he gained support and eventually he met with success. "The wording for a victim's rights amendment," he comments, "after being unanimously approved by both the house and the senate, will appear on my state's general ballot in the next election."

While Chet was battling to have a victim's rights amendment added to his state's constitution, he encountered defense lawyers who vehemently opposed the amendment. "These lawyers," he explains, "argued that juries might become prejudiced against those accused of crimes if they are informed of the devastating impact the crimes have had on the lives of the victims and their families."

That an accused criminal is given the opportunity to speak on his or her own behalf while victims—or in the case of a murder the victim's grieving family—are not allowed to speak, enhances the rage with which Chet is attempting to cope. He attributes his involvement in victim's rights issues with helping him to contain his rage and to survive his sons' deaths. "The work I am doing," he states, "helps keep me sane."

Chet's efforts to ensure that the rights of victims are guaranteed and protected, not only by his state government but by the federal government as well, recently took him to Washington, D.C. "One day I received a call from the General Counsel of the House Judiciary Committee," he says. "A push is on to have a victim's rights amendment added to the United States Constitution. I was invited to speak before the House Judiciary Committee. So I got in my car and headed north." After Chet and two other parents of murdered children spoke, two-thirds of the delegates present said they would support a victim's rights amendment. This show of support, although it did little to alleviate his pain, proved to Chet that his hard work and effort have not been in vain.

The parents of murdered children who engage in activities aimed at making changes in our criminal justice systems each have a specific goal in mind. Melanie's nineteen-year-old son was ambushed and gunned down by the seventeen-year-old, former boyfriend of a girl Melanie's son was dating. "The boy who killed my son was tried as an adult and was found guilty of first-degree, premeditated murder," she explains. "He is now serving a life sentence. But he could be paroled in about thirteen years."

Knowing that the boy who painstakingly planned and carried out her son's murder will someday be eligible for parole causes Melanie great anguish. So does the knowledge that the fifteen-year-old boy who provided the gun and took part in the ambush was tried by the juvenile system rather than by the adult system. "At the moment, he is in a facility for juvenile delinquents," she says. "Who knows for how long." Melanie believes that this boy should have been tried as an adult. "Because he was not," she continues, "I am attempting to change some laws, especially in the juvenile system."

Like Chet, Melanie's work to bring about change in the criminal justice system helps keep her sane. It also helps her to focus on the future and to manage her grief. "But," she states, "even though I'm so active doesn't mean that I'll ever recover."

Other parents, as part of working their way through the grieving process, and as a way to protect their sanity, also begin campaigns to change existing laws, or to have stronger ones enacted. After her son was shot to death in 1975, Lois began working to have stricter gun-control legislation enacted in her home state. Thirteen grueling years later she was successful; a law was passed banning the sale of cheap, poorly made handguns known as Saturday Night Specials.

Devoting thirteen years of one's life to banning the sale of only one type of handgun might seem incomprehensible to some people. But to Lois it is not. "I live each day with the scars of a handgun attack," she explains. "The loss of my son is forever. The emptiness is permanent."

Lois' effort to raise awareness for the need for stricter gun-control legislation has not been confined only to her home state. She has also spoken before the platform committees of two Democratic National Conventions. Lois' willingness to devote so much time and energy to a cause that she hopes will save the lives of many children, has not gone unnoticed. In July of 1989 she was featured in a *Newsweek* article praising the work of unsung heroes from across the United States.

While some parents choose to control their rage by working to make changes in our criminal justice systems, others choose to control theirs by joining organizations established to reduce crime. Janetta's thirty-year-old son and a friend were driving in the friend's car to a convenience store located in the neighborhood where Janetta and her family were residing at that time. The two young men made a wrong turn and found themselves trapped in the middle of a gang fight. Before they could escape, Janetta's son was shot and killed. After her son's death, Janetta joined a coalition formed to stop the violence occurring in her neighborhood. "The members of our coalition watched for violent activity, took pictures, and documented what they saw," she states. "We tried to get as many people involved as we could, including the Councilman for our district. And we made our activities known by getting the media involved."

Although being a member of the coalition was very painful for Janetta, she endured the pain because she needed to create positive change out of the chaos of violence. Knowing the devastating affect her son's murder has had on her and on her daughters, she has come to believe that, "No one should have to tolerate any kind of violence in their neighborhood. Public safety should be twenty-four hours a day."

Because the parents know first hand the permanent trauma a murder causes, it is not unusual for them to funnel their agony into activities that will protect other families from violence. Melanie hopes to prevent the murders of other young people by telling the story of her son's murder to teenagers in her community. "I try to make them aware of the effects of violence by speaking to them in their schools," she says.

Jenny is also attempting to increase awareness of the devastating effects of violence by participating in a victim awareness education program. This program organizes panels consisting of three survivors of violent crimes and arranges for them to speak to prisoners who are about to be paroled or who have been paroled. "The panel," explains Jenny, "can be made up of a person whose child has been sexually or physically abused, a rape survivor, and a person like me whose child was murdered. All types of violent crime are represented. We might speak to a group of three or four sex offenders or even murderers, but the nature of their crimes are not revealed to us."

The content of the message each panel member hopes to impart is chosen by the speakers themselves. "For instance," continues Jenny, "I tell my story from beginning to end, how the effects of the crime extend beyond the crime, and how my life and the lives of my family have changed."

Overall, Jenny has found that sitting on a panel has been a worthwhile experience. "The offenders to whom I have spoken have been, for the most part, respectful," she says. "Sometimes, though, I have to tell myself that these offenders are not the ones responsible for my daughter's murder, and that I cannot let my anger take over." Jenny is proud of the fact that the criminals who have been through the program have a lower rate of recidivism, and that those who do eventually commit other crimes, commit ones that are less serious than the ones they originally committed. "Although it is too late for me and my daughter," she comments, "I feel that if I can get the message across to one violent offender, I will have been successful."

In addition to working with the victim awareness education program, Jenny is the Program Director for the organization "Mothers Against Violence in America." "This group," she says, "works to reduce violence in our society. I became involved because I wanted to work on the prevention of youth violence."

When Mothers Against Violence in America was founded in January of 1994, it established three goals:

1. to build a network of informed advocates to promote the safety and well-being of children and youth,
2. to support local, state, and national efforts to prevent violence by and against youth, and
3. to promote educational efforts that give children and parents tools to deal with conflict nonviolently and that will change attitudes and behavior away from violence and toward civility.

Since its inception, the group has become highly visible and very active. It meets its goals in a wide variety of ways including presenting workshops and conferences aimed at finding solutions to the violence occurring in homes, schools, and neighborhoods. It also developed a speaker's bureau that sends speakers to local organizations interested in stemming youth violence, and it holds community meetings that educate and motivate people to become committed to finding solutions to violence.

"Mothers Against Violence in America also sponsors a student initiated organization, Students Against Violence Everywhere," continues Jenny. "I help young people organize chapters of this group in their schools. And I do much public speaking to students regarding how they must be involved in the solution process."

While the reduction or prevention of crime becomes the life work of parents like Melanie and Jenny, there are also parents who dedicate themselves to solving crimes by joining organizations designed to fulfill this function. Chet has been an active member of the organization "Crimestoppers" for several years. "When my second-oldest son was murdered in 1992 there were no witnesses to the crime, and no clues," he explains. "The case was solved with the aid of tips phoned in to Crimestoppers."

Each chapter of this international organization is made up of both police officers and civilians. From a general fund kept solvent by donations from civic groups, corporations, and individuals, it offers monetary rewards to persons who supply information about hard-to-solve crimes. The group is successful in solving crimes because all informants are guaranteed anonymity, and because rewards are given for information leading to the arrest of the person or persons who committed the crime.

Another important way in which some parents help themselves to survive the horror of their child's murder is by becoming personally involved with victims of crime and with their families. Pam is one of these parents. "After my daughter was murdered during a robbery in her home," she says, "I became a Victim Services Assistant at a victim services center."

The center offers eight separate and distinct services ranging from counseling victims and their families, to assisting victims in filing claims for State financial benefits for reimbursement of medical and psychological expenses, lost wages, and funeral expenses, to ensuring that victims are informed of their rights. Each service is described in a brochure that is circulated throughout Pam's community. "It is the mission of the Victim Services Center," states Pam, "to provide quality, comprehensive services to crime victims and survivors and their significant others, to reduce victims' trauma, and facilitate their recovery from the impact of victimization while advocating for their welfare and rights to fair treatment."

Becoming a Victim Services Assistant has helped Pam cope with her daughter's death. "And," she comments, "it is also my way of keeping my daughter alive. I have many opportunities to tell my story. In September of 1995, Attorney General Janet Reno visited our center and I told her about my daughter's murder."

Having the opportunity to tell how their child died, and becoming involved in activities that help keep the memory of their child alive, are but two of the reasons parents of murdered children become active in organizations that aid victims. They also become active as a way to reconstruct their shattered lives. "I was referred to the organization "Families and Friends of Violent Crime Victims and Missing persons" by the prosecutor's office within a couple of weeks of my daughter's murder," explains Jenny. "The group, formed in 1975 as a crime victim support and advocacy group, has been most helpful in the reconstruction of my life."

Family and Friends of Violent Crime Victims and Missing Persons provides services designed to be of use to victims of all types of crime. These services include twenty-four hour availability, one-on-one crisis intervention, peer support group meetings, courtroom support, resources, referrals, and education services to crime victims and their loved ones. The organization also matches empathetic volunteers and former victims with the people it serves. "I was so grateful for the support given me and my family," Jenny continues, "that eighteen months after my daughter's murder I decided I wanted to be trained as a volunteer victim advocate with Family and Friends in order that I might help someone else going through this horror. I took extensive training in the education area regarding victimization issues and continue to do so presently."

Survival is a goal shared by all parents of a murdered child. For many of them survival is a two-phase process. During phase one the parents seek out persons, such as family members and close friends, who are willing to give them support. If the support they receive is inadequate or sporadic, they then seek out groups offering a full range of support functions that are both stable and constant.

"One of the most important services offered by Family and Friends is its monthly support group," states Jenny. "My husband and myself began attending their support group where we met other survivor's of homicide victims. Those in attendance were not limited only to parents. There were brothers, sisters, grandparents, cousins, best friends, classmates, etc. It was such a relief to know that my reactions, both emotionally and physically, were normal. And that I was not going crazy!"

The fear of becoming insane is one of the most torturous aspects of murdered-child grief. It is a fear that only another parent of a murdered child can comprehend completely. Newly bereaved parents can only gain a full understanding of it by talking with parents who have also suffered the murder of their child. Unfortunately, this fear is only one of the many painful emotions that threaten to overwhelm the parents. Eventually they must gain a full understanding of each emotion in order to ensure their survival. Many parents choose to do this by joining homicide bereavement support groups.

In addition to their need to understand the glut of emotions tormenting them, most parents find that they have an ongoing need to talk about their child's murder, the criminal justice system, and their grief. This ongoing need is another reason many parents join homicide bereavement support groups.

Rose, when her twenty-two-year-old son was beaten to death by his college roommate, became a member of the organization "Parents of Murdered Children and Other Survivors of Homicide Victims" (POMC). "I joined this organization for grief support and judicial support," she explains.

POMC, as it is commonly referred to by its members, is comprised of well-organized, highly effective chapters operating in states all across the country. In addition to holding monthly meetings, each chapter publishes a monthly newsletter that is distributed to its members. These newsletters provide important information ranging from how to deal with parole boards and parole hearings, to legislative updates, to whom to telephone when a member needs immediate emotional support. It also publishes poems and stories written by chapter members in honor of their murdered loved ones.

The newsletter is extremely important, especially to those members of POMC who cannot attend the monthly meetings. Via its contents, they can share in the grief emotions expressed by other survivors, come to understand their own feelings of grief, and keep current on homicide-related events occurring in the criminal justice system in their community.

The philosophy of Parents of Murdered Children and Other Survivors of Homicide Victims is comforting yet straightforward. The one that follows was taken from the newsletter of POMC's Central Ohio Chapter:

> We are sorry for the circumstances that bring you to our group, but we hope that we can be of some assistance to you as you work through your grief. Our meetings are open to any survivor of a homicide victim—Parent, Brother, Sister, Cousin, Aunt, Uncle, Grandparent, Son, Daughter, Friend, etc. You are invited to attend our meetings each month. Nothing is required of you. There are no dues or fees and you need not speak a word. Attending your first meeting takes courage, but most find it a comforting network of support, friendship, and understanding that only those who have been there can give. We welcome everyone. The meetings are a time for sharing stories, experiences, and emotions. We share a common bond, so we are free to express any emotion: anger, sadness, frustration, and sometimes even laughter.

In 1982, after Elsie's daughter was stabbed to death during a robbery in the daughter's home, Elsie became a member of Parents of Murdered Children. "Group involvement is the greatest way to start the healing process," she comments. "It is a safe place to talk and no one will judge you."

"When I joined Parents of Murdered Children," adds Evelyn, "I found that I could talk and all understood and listened. They didn't judge me."

It is not surprising that Elsie, Evelyn, and a large number of other grieving parents, seek out the counsel and companionship of those who will not judge them. Sadly, after a child is murdered, some people place blame on the parents rather than on the killer. They infer that the parents failed to protect their child. Or that they failed to provide a strong home life or proper discipline. As stated in a previous chapter, this is done, I believe, out of fear. These people think that if they take excellent care of their own children and continually monitor their activities, they can eliminate any possibility of one of their children being murdered. This judgmental attitude, or assessment of blame, is another reason many parents seek the safety and comfort of homicide bereavement support groups.

Phase two of the parents' struggle to survive begins when they have successfully completed a partial reconstruction of their lives and have reduced their grief to a manageable level. Even though their lives will never again be the same, and even though they will always feel grief, they have reached the point where they can begin helping other bereaved parents by passing along the same kind of empathy, guidance, and support that was given to them.

Mata, whose twenty-one-year-old daughter was kidnapped and brutally murdered by a man the daughter refused to date, entered phase two when she joined a chapter of Parents of Murdered Children. "My joining POMC was my lifesaver," comments Mata. "I found that if I worked with other people like me, I was able to cope."

Margie is also a member of POMC. "My husband and I are active members in our chapter," she says. "It gives us such strength, hope, and the chance to help others."

With each passing day murder rates increase across our country, and more and more persons are faced with the overwhelming task of surviving the murder of a loved one. This increase has alerted former survivors, medical doctors, and mental health professionals to the need for knowledgeable and compassionate support for survivors. Often they respond to this need by establishing homicide bereavement support groups.

An example of this is the group sponsored by the Hospice of the Chesapeake located in central Maryland. The group's facilitator, a psychologist who lost a nephew to murder several years ago, conducts monthly sharing sessions, and presents programs on understanding and managing the emotions homicide survivors experience as well as speakers who are familiar with the traumas of homicide-related grief.

This psychologist, perhaps because she is a homicide survivor, is an excellent facilitator. Her demeanor is calm and accepting. She asks a minimal number of questions designed to encourage participants to voice their true feelings of grief, and while they are speaking she does not interrupt with comments or opinions of her own. When one group member is speaking with another, she does not interfere in their conversation. With her, group members know they can freely express their rage with the killer and with the criminal justice system. She provides a safe and non-judgmental environment in which all persons can speak openly and honestly, but she never forces anyone to speak if they do not want to. One of the most valuable services this psychologist provides to members of the group is inviting the Director of the Victim-Witness Assistance Program who works out of the State's Attorney's office to every meeting. Having the Director at each meeting makes new attendees aware of the program, gives them an opportunity to ask questions about the services the program provides to survivors of violent crime, and to explain problems they are having with any branch of the criminal justice system. This homicide bereavement support group is a valuable asset to the residents of central Maryland. Those who participate return to it again, and again, and again.

Grieving individuals who participate in bereavement support groups on an ongoing basis eventually find that reaching out to newly bereaved parents helps them to cope with their own grief. "Active involvement," explains Beckie, "helps keep us sane, gives meaning to our pain, and to our children's lives."

Engaging in activities that bring about change in our criminal justice systems and help reduce violence in our society, joining organizations that aid victims and protect victims' rights, and participating in bereavement support groups are not the only ways in which the parents of murdered children survive their grief. They also look to the future. When looking to the future, the parents create situations, or take part in events, that will ultimately help others in grief.

In 1987, the executive director of the "National Parents of Murdered Children Organization" created what has come to be known as "The Memorial Wall." Designed by a member of POMC, this portable wall, inscribed with the names, dates of birth, and dates of death of homicide victims, continually travels throughout the United States so that it can be put on display for all to see. The purpose of The Memorial Wall is twofold. It gives homicide survivors the opportunity to honor their deceased loved ones in a significant and permanent way. And it gives members of society the opportunity to see that murder victims are much more than nameless statistics, as well as the tragic number of murders that have occurred in our country.

After their son was murdered, Carol and her husband Jim founded a chapter of POMC. In addition, they filed and won a wrongful death suit against the man who murdered their son. "Our son's murderer," explains Carol, "must pay a percent of all future income to Parents of Murdered Children." This monetary commitment, although it might be small at times, symbolizes the desire Carol and Jim harbor to ensure that the support organization that helped them survive their grief will continue to function.

"I hope to someday open a teen center," adds Melanie, "with a support group for grieving teens. This will not only take lots of money, but I will need a building. I am in hopes that someone will donate a building. Even though it will not bring my boy back, my energy must go towards positive things."

Many parents also hope to educate those who have not experienced murdered-child grief on the devastating effect violence of any kind has on victims and their families. In 1994, when Chet was invited to appear on a segment of the television show, "Nightline," his initial response was, "Absolutely not!" Then, because the segment centered around prisons and the rehabilitation of convicted criminals, he overcame his nervousness at being on national television and agreed to participate. "I only contributed about thirty seconds worth of commentary," says Chet, "but in that thirty seconds I was able to get the point across that rehabilitation works only if it comes from within. All the tax money, efforts, and classes won't help an inmate unless he wants to be rehabilitated."

A few years ago a Hollywood writer/producer contacted Rose to discuss the possibility of doing a television movie detailing her son's murder. Although she knew that participating in such a project would cause her great pain, Rose agreed to do it. Because her son had been murdered by his best friend and college roommate, it was important to her that all members of society realize that murder can occur at any time and in any place, and that no one, regardless of their status in life, is ever exempt. This movie titled "What Happened to Bobby Earl" was completed in 1996, and was aired on national television in early 1997.

* * *

During recent political campaigns on all levels of government, the issue of violent crime has been high on the list of major concerns. Because of this, the media, including radio and television talk shows, are expressing a greater interest in how survivors of violent crimes are dealing with their trauma.

One of the questions most often asked parents of murdered children is, "How did you cope with the loss of your child?" As you can see, all parents cope differently. They begin by making a commitment to surviving their grief and to reconstructing their lives. Then they move forward by reaching out to others in need in ways that best suit their individual personalities.

If you are the parent of a murdered child who is struggling to cope with your grief, but are not sure how to go about it, acquaint yourself with the groups and organizations in your area that help bereaved persons, and/or victims of violent crime. These groups and organizations are listed in your telephone directory and in books available at your local library. Do not hesitate to contact one or more of these groups to inquire about the services and programs they offer. Because many of their staff members have walked in your shoes, they will be happy to speak with you.

This same advice applies to those of you who are committed to helping the parents of a murdered child to survive their terrible grief. The more information you have about the services available to these parents, and about murdered-child grief, the better able you will be to assist them on the long road to reconstructing their lives.

Summary

> If I can help ease the pain of another parent then my sons will not have died for nothing.
>
> *Chet*
> *1-23-96*

Of the three grief books I have written, this one caused me the most pain. It rekindled frustrations and feelings of murdered-child grief I thought I had resolved years ago. The research I did made me realize that murder occurs all too frequently in every segment of society. It made me see violence, and its devastating effects, in a glaringly bright light that casts no shadow.

The purpose of my writing is to tell the truth about grief; to describe the emotions felt by the parents of a murdered child regardless of how terrifying or repugnant these emotions are. I can honestly say that I wonder how some parents are managing to stay sane. The horrors of their situations are so pernicious and cataclysmic I wonder why they have not snapped and retaliated against their child's killer, their criminal justice system, or their legislature.

You might think that my words are overly harsh and truculent. And perhaps they are. But when you consider that the murder of the parents' priceless creation is also harsh and truculent, you can understand why I use them.

Parents who have survived their child's murder are forced to carry a burden that no human should ever be expected to carry. Most of the time they carry this burden with dignity. But when they do not—when, for a moment, their emotions of rage and agony erupt and spew forth—some people turn away from them.

How do the parents of a murdered child manage to carry their burden of grief? Why don't they snap under the weight of the emotions that torment them and turn upon their child's killer or the criminal justice system that seems to favor violent offenders rather than victims? The answer is this. The parents are decent people who do not believe that violence can be rectified with violence. Rather than debase themselves by breaking the law, they choose to change the law. And they are strong. They "dig in their heels" and begin the painful process of reconstructing their lives. They fight to overcome their grief, and they fight for survival using weapons that are unique to them. Along the way, they depend on themselves, their family and friends, and other people with whom they come in contact. Although these people might not comprehend the magnitude of murdered-child grief, many of them do reach out to the grieving parents.

Knowing that the parents will never forget their child, these people provide an environment conducive to keeping the child's memory alive. They encourage the parents to speak freely. They hear what the parents are saying. They do not judge, and they do not assess blame. They continue to associate with the parents, no matter how painful and upsetting that association is. They devise ways to help the parents reconstruct their shattered lives. They remain steadfast and true. And in doing so they lessen the weight of the burden the parents are carrying.

These people urge the parents to listen to what is in their hearts and to act accordingly. If their hearts tell them to visit the cemetery daily, they do not accuse them of obsessing over their grief. If their hearts tell them to put together a scrapbook of their child's death, they do not think the parents are being morbid. They accept the parents' behaviors as being necessary to their survival.

They encourage the parents to join bereavement support groups, not because they want to be rid of the parents, but because they know that members of these groups can be empathetic rather than just sympathetic. They uphold the parents' decision to become active members of organizations devoted to expanding victims' rights, or to making changes in our criminal justice systems. If the parents become involved in a time-consuming campaign to reduce violence in their community, or to raise awareness of the devastating affect violence has on society, they help out in any way they can.

These people gain some understanding of murdered-child grief by reading books or by speaking with facilitators of bereavement support groups. They put aside their own feelings of fear and discomfort because they know that what the parents are feeling is a thousand times worse. They realize that the help they give will require them to be courageous. And they know that they cannot expect the parents to be courageous in their battle to survive unless they are as well.

They stick with the parents during the worst of their grief. And when the going gets rough, as it definitely does, they strengthen their resolve to stand by the parents.

Violence affects everyone. It reduces the quality of our lives and increases the taxes and health insurance premiums we pay. It causes us to feel unsafe in our homes and in our communities. It offends our sense of morality. It dishonors and debases us. It adds to the complexity and trauma of murdered-child grief.

Murdered-child grief is difficult for both the parents and those who come in contact with them to understand. After the murder, the parents change in many ways. It is impossible for them to walk through the devastating hell of their grief and come through unscathed. This does not mean that they are incapable of reconstructing their lives, in spite of the pain they continue to suffer. But the reconstruction process requires time, courage, and determination. It also requires the continuing support and patience of all who associate with the parents either personally or professionally.

If you are the parent of a murdered child, I hope the feelings of grief expressed in this book make you feel less alone and less frightened. If you are someone who is struggling to interact with the parents of a murdered child, I hope you now have some understanding of what they are feeling, why they are feeling that way, and how you can help them.

Index

Part One
GENERAL GRIEF

Part Two
MURDERED-CHILD GRIEF

About the Author

The youngest of three sisters, Bonnie was born on October 15, 1941 in Baltimore, Maryland, and has lived in a variety of environments including urban, suburban, and rural.

In 1959, at age seventeen, she married her high school sweetheart. They have been married for thirty-eight years. During the first five of those thirty-eight years she gave birth to two daughters and one son. She is also the proud grandmother of five grandchildren.

Her love of reading led her to a love of writing. After studying creative writing, she freelanced for the *Baltimore Sun* newspaper as a human interest reporter.

When her youngest daughter was shot to death in 1983, she became interested in grief and the grieving process as it relates to bereaved parents. Her interest resulted in her writing two books on grief. The first, *When a Child Has Died: Ways You Can Help a Bereaved Parent,* was published by Fithian Press in 1995. The second, *Who Will Sing to Me Now?* was published by Books Unlimited in 1996.

Made in the USA
Las Vegas, NV
23 March 2021

20068205R00090